HOUSEPLANTS

The American Horticultural Society
Illustrated Encyclopedia of Gardening

HOUSEPLANTS

The American Horticultural Society
Mount Vernon, Virginia

For The American Horticultural Society

President
Dr. Gilbert S. Daniels

Technical Advisory Committee
Dr. Henry M. Cathey
Everett Conklin
Mary Stuart Maury

**Houseplants Staff for
The Franklin Library/Ortho Books**

Editorial Director
Min S. Yee

Supervisory Editor
Lewis P. Lewis

Editor
A. Cort Sinnes

Art Director
John A. Williams

Creative Director
Michael Mendelsohn

Contributing Writers
Thomas Downey
Elvin McDonald
James K. McNair
William C. Mulligan

Contributing Photographers
William Alpin
Ernest Braun
Clyde Childress
Tyler Childress
Charles Marden Fitch
Michael Landis
Fred Lyon
Elvin McDonald
Burt O'Neal

Illustrator
Ron Hildebrand

Production Director
Robert Laffler

Production Manager
Renee Guilmette

For Ortho Books

Publisher
Robert L. Iacopi

For The Franklin Library

Publisher
Joseph Sloves

The two houseplants shown on the cover are gloxinias *(Sinningia speciosa)* of the variety called 'Red Velvet'. Photographed by Clara Aich.

Produced under the authorization of The American Horticultural Society by The Franklin Library and Ortho Books.

Copyright © 1974, 1976, 1980 by Ortho Books. Special contents © 1980 by The American Horticultural Society. All rights reserved under International and Pan-American Copyright Conventions.

Every effort has been made at the time of publication to guarantee the accuracy of the names and addresses of information sources and suppliers and in the technical data contained. However, the subscriber should check for his own assurance and must be responsible for selection and use of suppliers and supplies, plant materials, and chemical products.

No portion of this book may be reproduced in any form or by any means without permission first being requested and obtained from The American Horticultural Society, c/o The Franklin Library, Franklin Center, Pennsylvania, 19091. Portions of this volume previously appeared in the Ortho Books *Houseplants Indoors/Outdoors* and *The Facts of Light about Indoor Gardening.*

Library of Congress Catalog Card Number 79-56428
Printed in the United States of America.

12 11 10 9 8

A Special Message from
The American Horticultural Society

One of the responsibilities of The American Horticultural Society to its members is making them aware of the best books on gardening, wherever these may appear. And in the process of fulfilling this assignment, we have long had the ambition of publishing a series of gardening books that would bear our own imprint. *The Illustrated Encyclopedia of Gardening* accomplishes that.

It seems right that one of the first volumes of our Encyclopedia should be about houseplants. In the past decade what for millions of people was merely a mild interest in houseplants has mushroomed into engrossing attachment, even affection. People love their plants, talk to their plants, watch television programs about plants or just plain enjoy their plants. Houseplants have indeed become something of a companion in life for a great many of us. All to the good. Growing houseplants satisfies a basic gardening urge. They invariably enhance their surroundings with their color, fragrance or foliage. (They also are healthy to have around since they help absorb noise pollution and purify the air we breathe.)

Caring for any houseplant can be tricky, but it shouldn't be complicated. Intelligent attention, proper care for that particular type of plant and the correct environment surrounding it are the three most important factors in keeping a plant healthy. All plants are originally native to an outside environment somewhere in the world, and the key to success with houseplants is in simulating their natural environment as closely as possible in your home or office.

And that is what *Houseplants* is all about. We have tried to make it the best guide to houseplant culture that is published. With accurate knowledge of each plant's habits and requirements, everyone should be able to keep houseplants successfully.

There are bound to be a few disappointments, however. Some will be mysterious, some predictable, but most explainable. The plant that you bought at a local garden center six months ago that flowered beautifully was *supposed* to wither and die gradually because it was a biennial and had already spent more than half its lifespan being grown at a nursery before it arrived at the garden center—and finally your house. On the other hand, perhaps the African violets died because they were left on a south window sill during the summer and were badly sunburned. There is reason and logic to it all. And that knowledge we hope to help you acquire.

This book tells you what to do, how to do it, when to do it, and is full of good advice and information about hundreds of plants. The proper soil, or the proper soilless soil, watering, repotting, the right containers, expectable dormancy, pruning and pinching, flowers, ferns, vegetables—it's all here, a thorough, thoughtful selection of what you need to know that will make keeping houseplants uncomplicated, satisfying and a genuine pleasure.

Gilbert S. Daniels
President

CONTENTS

When you landscape an indoor environment, there are several factors to take into consideration: the needs of the plants, the "climate" inside your house, the amount of sunlight that naturally enters the room, and how the sunlight changes from season to season. The most successful indoor gardeners know how these factors work together and how to coordinate a plant's needs with existing conditions.

The basics of growing plants indoors include selecting proper containers, meeting a plant's light and humidity requirements, knowing the fundamentals of soil, water and fertilizers, how and when to pot and repot plants, a few good grooming techniques, and knowing what to do when a plant develops a problem. This chapter also includes plans for a compact indoor potting shed for do-it-yourselfers.

Using Natural Light   40

Practically every indoor environment receives some natural light, even if it isn't direct sunlight. All plants need light to grow, and the more you know about light in general, and about the light that enters your house in particular, the better an indoor gardener you will be. This chapter also offers ways to measure the light indoors, plants lists for various exposures, and ways to modify natural light.

Using Artificial Light   62

If there still isn't enough light for all the plants you want to grow, you may want to also use artificial light. This chapter explores many alternatives for gardening indoors under lights, the difference between incandescent and fluorescent light, and available manufactured fixtures and equipment. Even if the sun doesn't shine on your plants, they can still grow well.

Miniature Gardens   74

Terrariums originally were invented to transport living plants from the far parts of the world. Today's terrariums are more decorative in nature, but they still allow you to have a little garden that can be maintained for long periods of time with a minimum amount of attention. This chapter contains all the necessary information for creating these miniature landscapes.

Flowering Houseplants 78

For many indoor gardeners, the ultimate achievement is getting a plant to bloom "in captivity." Selecting several species of blooming plants lets you have container plants flowering year-round. This chapter includes an encyclopedia of both familiar and unusual flowering houseplants—from African violets to the Zebra plant. Also included are flowering bulbs which can be grown as houseplants.

Foliage Houseplants 90

Foliage houseplants form the backbone of most indoor gardens. Their infinite variations in leaf shape, color, and texture let you put together beautiful plant collections and combinations. From miniature plants to those that grow to specimen proportions, this chapter supplies all the information you need to select and care for the plants you like best. Read, learn, and then take your pick.

Shrubs as Houseplants 106

Not all shrubs have to be grown in permanent outdoor locations. Many can grow indoors indefinitely in containers, and then be moved outdoors (and vice versa), as your particular climate dictates. Most shrubs you can grow indoors represent a good value, in terms of their size and dramatic effect. This chapter considers some of the shrubs that are best suited to indoor/outdoor container culture.

Cacti and Other Succulents 114

Cacti and other succulents represent a special group of plants of particular interest to indoor gardeners. For the most part, they are well-suited for indoor container gardening—virtually all cacti and other succulents have the ability to exist, if not thrive, in the normally dry, warm atmosphere of the average house. Once you get started collecting this varied group of plants, you may not be able to stop.

Propagating 120

Propagating plants at home is a good way to multiply your plant collection inexpensively. Almost every seed catalog offers seeds of the more common houseplants. This chapter tells how to plant seeds, care for seedlings, root cuttings, take leaf cuttings, propagate trees and shrubs from softwood and hardwood cuttings, and multiply by division. Also, it gives the how-to on stolon propagation.

Plant Selection Guide 128

Learn about the light requirements, best conditions, exposure, water requirements, and humidity and temperature levels for many houseplants and outdoor/indoor plants.

INTERIOR LANDSCAPING

Container gardening is easy, and the mobility of the plants makes it possible to rearrange your background whenever you wish.

Many people stumble onto the rewarding pleasure of container gardening when they receive a gift plant wrapped in foil and tied with a florist's bow. Suddenly you feel like the new parent of something alive. Don't panic! Just get rid of that foil and bow, and explore the fascinating world of houseplants.

Plants have been cultivated in containers for centuries, but only in the last decade or so has the idea really caught on. Today it seems that plant shops, florists and nurseries are on every corner. Even the supermarkets and department stores have sections devoted to green, growing things.

Commercial growers say that they find it difficult to grow plants fast enough to meet the demand. Specimen trees are becoming scarce. Growers are turning out small plants with almost assembly line speed, and it is even becoming difficult to locate some of the old favorite houseplants.

The fact is, we *need* living plants around us; they help purify the atmosphere, give us oxygen and absorb noise pollution.

A plant responds to the individual who cares for it. This doesn't mean you have to whisper sweet nothings to it, or play Bach or rock music for it. But it does mean that when you adopt a plant as your own, you become responsible for its well being. Plants that grow in the ground depend less on humans than those that grow in containers, which is partly why so many people are growing plants in pots today. They want to feel closer to nature, but not everyone wants to or can afford to go all the way back to the farm. All you need is one seed and a pot of moist soil and you can experience all the good things of plant life, nature's perfect cycle and the heady aroma of healthy soil.

Trends in Container Gardening

Growing all kinds of flowers, shrubs and trees in containers has always been a common procedure in estate gardens everywhere, and shortly after World War II the practice became generally popular in California. Slowly but surely it has spread over the entire country. People who wouldn't dream of committing their leisure time to a perennial flower border or a large lawn are eager to grow pots, tubs and baskets of plants in outdoor areas.

Prim rows of windowsill pots have given way to indoor trees with branches reaching over sofas and chairs. Instead of draperies at the windows, today we see hanging baskets in many homes and apartments. And in interior spaces where bright light or sun never reaches, fluorescent and cool-beam incandescent lights provide life-giving rays for plants.

Container gardening allows you to let your imagination run wild. Almost any plant can be grown in a container. You can have a miniature lawn with a flower border, a vegetable garden or a tree. Don't be afraid to try whatever strikes your fancy. Start with seed, young plants or full grown nursery stock. Remember that while you must select plant material that will do well where you plan to grow it, the plants themselves will modify the environment.

Above: **1.** The unusual flowers of the lipstick vine, *Aeschynanthus*. **2.** Variegated *Impatiens*. **3.** The Charles Foster Restaurant in Atlanta offers relaxing dining among potted trees. **4.** Most houseplants can be rooted in water and transplanted easily into soilless mixes. By starting plants in clear glass containers, you can see the root development as it progresses. The lower leaves of this *Dracaena marginata* were removed from the stem before placing it in water.

Travel has also influenced container gardening. Magnificent container gardens all over Europe have inspired us to do the same. And as more of us grow plants in containers, the demand has grown for a greater selection. Wholesale growers in warm-weather climates now find it profitable to propagate more unusual plants, and daily these are trucked or air-freighted all over the country. The *Carissa*, or Natal plum, that flowers and bears fruit in a container in Florida on Friday may well be found in a retail nursery in Minnesota the following week. Shortly thereafter, it will be taken home to be planted in a handsome terra-cotta pot or possibly turned into a bonsai. In this northern climate it will spend the summer outdoors, the winter indoors. This indoor-outdoor mobility of container plants is one theme of this book.

What Is a Houseplant?

Nature does not grow any "houseplants" as such. All plants grown in containers indoors are native to an outdoor environment somewhere. Given favorable atmospheric conditions, almost anything that grows can be a houseplant.

The revolution in plant distribution makes it possible to enjoy plants native to other habitats in almost any climate. You can grow exotic bulbs in and out of season. You can plant herbs and vegetables, not only to reap the harvest, but

Right: Sometimes called *Dipladenia*, *Mandevilla splendens* is a rapid-growing evergreen vine loaded with clusters of large pink flowers against leathery dark green leaves.

also for the beauty of their foliage and flowers and the enjoyment of their fragrance.

Citrus and other fruit-bearing trees can provide people everywhere with a year-round orangery. Arid desert species grow on window sills thousands of miles from the desert. Many outdoor shrubs and vines can be grown indoors, or, better yet, grown both indoors and outdoors, depending on weather conditions. Plants our grandparents have never heard of are available from specialty growers or importers through local outlets or mail order. (Check the source list on page 139.)

With careful selection, houseplants can be combined effectively with the overall decor. The plants shown above were chosen for their leaf color and plant habit and blend pleasingly with the kitchen memorabilia.

Creating the Proper Environment

Houses are built to give their owners a more comfortable climate. More often than not, the indoor climate is characterized by low humidity and a temperature in the low 70s—not exactly ideal conditions for growing plants. On the other hand, if you wanted to grow perfect houseplants you could convert your living room into a greenhouse—the plants would thrive and the people would suffer. In between these two extremes a climate can be created in which both people and plants can live comfortably under the same roof—all it takes is an understanding of an average indoor climate and the requirements of growing plants in this alien environment.

Houses have different atmospheres; the one in your home should help you to determine which plants to grow and how to care for them. We cannot tell you what to grow, but want to offer you a wide selection, along with basic gardening guidelines. Find what works for you, with the resources you have available—indoors or outdoors—for growing plants in containers. Whether you want to grow one tomato plant in a pot or a whole garden full, you will find all the "how-to" information in this book, along with ideas for many plants you can grow and ways to enjoy them.

Plants belong in every room (there's even a reason to put poinsettias in the closet. See page 85), and there are comparatively few real restrictions. Plants that live indoors must survive in an artificial environment—one considerably different than their native habitat. Few living rooms have the Mediterranean climate from which the Jerusalem cherry originates, the tropical climate of philodendrons or the desert environment that nurtures succulents. The artificial atmosphere in which plants indoors are asked to thrive differs from their native habitat in significant ways:

☐ a home environment tends to have a relatively constant temperature and low humidity;

☐ pots restrict root growth, and the soil they contain fluctuates in fertility and moisture;

☐ there is little or no air movement or rain to refresh plant foliage;

☐ watering, unlike natural rainfall, is often of poor quality and usually too much or too little;

☐ feeding tends to be concentrated;

But particularly:

☐ light is generally from one direction:

☐ darkness is of a shorter duration (assimilation of nutrients takes place during dark hours);

And emphatically:

☐ there is usually much less light in the normal indoor situation.

Light and the Indoor Environment

We hope that the ideas described on the following pages will stimulate you to try gardening in indoor areas you would never have considered before. The fact is, with a little imagination almost any lighting problem can be solved. Estimating the amount of light available for plant growth is essential in order to select the right plants and to place them in the proper settings. Several techniques will be described to measure light levels or to approximate light intensity.

We'll name names—both common and botanical—of houseplants, with the lighting requirements necessary for healthy growth. It may seem unnecessary, but botanical names are carefully given and frequently used throughout this book because common names of many plants vary regionally while botanical names are used the world over, and guarantee immediate and positive identification. Plants that can take direct sunlight will be pointed out, as well as those that can survive in usually dim northern light. Long-day and short-day plants will be identified, along with a description of the special care they need.

Artificial light is man-made sun—it can make a tropical garden bloom in an area devoid of natural light. It can be used as a supplement to natural sunlight or as a sole light source.

You can anticipate the seasons with indoor container projects; summer vegetable and flower gardens can be started indoors during the winter and early spring. Seedlings can be grown stronger and faster under artificial light.

This book also contains ideas about how to design or remodel homes to receive the best advantages of light, making indoor gardening not only successful, but also an indispensable part of the home environment.

For people who have overflowing collections of plants, space can be a problem. Here, extra growing space was achieved in a bathroom by using a greenhouse window. The orchids thrive with the extra humidity. Far right: the owners of this house took advantage of a remodeling project to increase the amount of sunlight they receive. The final result? A combination greenhouse, sun room, and dining room.

These pages show the ultimate in a setting for indoor gardening—a Northern California redwood house designed by David Clayton for a couple who wanted a "perfect" environment for their extensive plant collection. Many skylights and windows of every shape and size were incorporated into the design to capture as much natural light as possible. Attention was given to details that make indoor gardening easier: a greenhouse, a potting shed entrance, terracotta floors that water can't damage, pulleys to lower plants for watering and special places for wet plants to drain.

Consider the plants you will want around you when you design or remodel a space for living or working. And think about incorporating some of the good ideas you will find here into a new or modified environment.

Conflicting Advice to Indoor Gardeners

Indoor gardeners are often baffled by so much available information. This excerpt from an editorial by Dr. H. M. Cathey, in *American Nurseryman*, may help to clarify some of the conflicting advice you receive.

If you assemble more than one gardener in the room and begin discussing the care, feeding and sunlight requirements of any species of plant, you'll soon find an argument in the brewing. Even the environmental requirements of a simple plant like a coleus may start a raging controversy. Although most gardeners will agree that filtered sun is best, very few individuals can come to an agreement about the proper

3

4

5

This redwood house designed by David Clayton is located in a quiet, wooded retreat overlooking the Pacific Ocean. Every day isn't as perfectly clear as the one captured in these photos, and the owners wanted a space where they could grow plants in spite of the prevailing fog. Thus the decision to open up the house to allow in as much sunlight as possible. **1.** The architecture features skylights and many windows of all sizes and shapes. Guests enter the house through a combination greenhouse-potting shed, passing through a conservatory of specimen plants. **2.** The conservatory, to the right of the entryway, has terracotta floors with drains, making plant watering an easy job. **3** and **4.** Hanging plants are bathed from the top in eastern sunlight by small skylights. Extended windows below them provide ample light as the sun shifts throughout the day. All of the hanging pots in the house have temporary, clamp-on plastic bowls to catch spills or drainage. They are made from plastic food containers attached with wire hooks made from coat hangers. **5.** Plants in the bathroom are grouped on a built-in ledge underneath a trapezoid shaped window that follows the lines of the roof. This tends to tie the indoor and outdoor foliage together. The tropical plants enjoy the additional humidity from running faucets and an adjoining steam room and Jacuzzi.

Plants can thrive in the bathroom, especially when there is sufficient light. H. Judd Wirz and Associates designed this cool, humid retreat for plants and people.

fertilizer and moisture levels for these relatively hardy plants.

Check any gardening book to examine our current state of knowledge. Read and compare the suggested frequency of the watering of a Norfolk Island pine or a Bosten fern. Now check another source. You will note that one suggests that you water almost daily; others encourage you to train the plant and water it only once a week. Now, mix and stir these views with other monographs written by noted garden authorities and you will find hundreds of opinions on syringing, the proper fertilizer, the correct sun exposure, the best way to control insects, proper pruning methods, propagation techniques . . . etc. The opinions are endless and, oddly enough, to a degree, may be correct.

If we draw a conclusion from all these noted authorities, we discover that plants are extremely tolerant of a wide range of abuse from the cultural procedures to which we subject them . . . plants adjust their growth characteristics and survive often under the most difficult conditions. Yet many plants will die abruptly if too much abuse is given them. Others just slowly "do the strip"—as one leaf after another falls from the plant.

Most gardeners take their failures in stride. They simply try again . . . and again . . . and again, often reading every monograph they can find on the subject. Eventually they profit from their previous mistakes of not enough light, moisture or nutrients. Eternal optimism rules the mind of the good gardeners.

The aim of this book is to profit from good indoor gardening practices learned from good indoor gardeners.

Indoor Seasons

The changing seasons have an immediate effect on the indoor environment. The amount of light that enters rooms through windows increases after the winter solstice (December 22) and decreases after the summer solstice (June 22). The angle of direct sunlight changes as the sun moves north in the spring and south in the fall. Since the winter sun is lower in the sky, plants that may have received only indirect light in the summer may be sunlit in the winter. As lighting conditions change, plants will become "out of focus." To make up for this change in light, shift indoor plants as the seasons change. Plants that grow well in an eastern or southern window in the summer will probably like a western exposure best in the winter. Plants that require the brightest light may require supplementary artificial illumination in the winter in order to maintain robust health.

Redecorating with Plants by Seasons

Move your plants as well as furnishings according to the season. Here is a hypothetical living room (shown without doors and with windows facing all four directions) illustrating what may be done with each exposure in each season.

Key: A. Sofa & chairs **B.** Coffee table **C.** Fireplace hearth & mantle **D.** Table **E.** Christmas tree

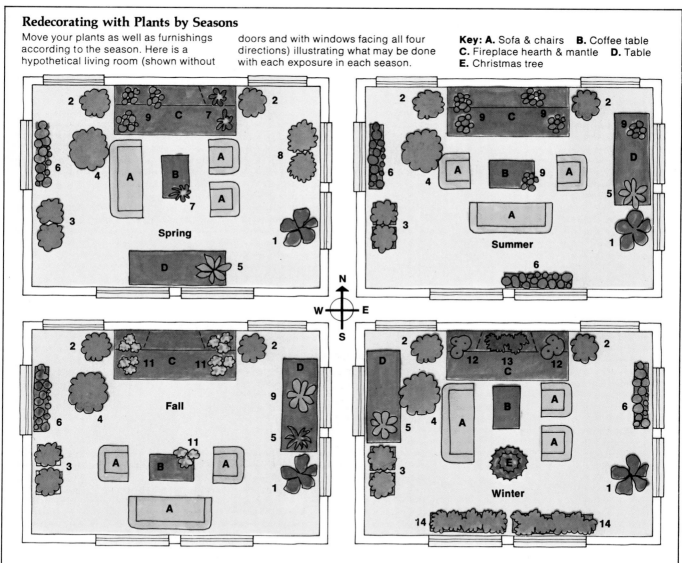

PLANTS: **1.** Fiddle leaf fig (*Ficus lyrata*) takes direct, filtered sun from the east all year. **2.** Cast iron plant (*Aspidistra elatior*) takes low light of northern exposure. **3.** Hawaiian ti (*Cordyline terminalis*) thrives in southwestern exposure with bright, not direct sun. **4.** Weeping fig (*Ficus benjamina*) needs bright, indirect light; might drop leaves if moved. **5.** Mother-in-law's tongue (*Sansevieria* species) takes any exposure. **6.** Cactus and succulent collection can take full sun from the south and west in summer. **7.** Bulbs in containers moved indoors need no special light while in bloom. **8.** Budding azaleas brought indoors will bloom in direct eastern sun. **9.** Cut flowers from garden add color. **10.** Thanksgiving cactus (*Schlumbergera truncatus*) needs filtered or diffused sunlight. **11.** Container chrysanthemums in bloom, brought indoors, need no special light. **12.** Poinsettias forced into bloom at Christmas. **13.** Jerusalem Cherry (*Solanum pseudocapsicum*) may be brought indoors while blooming at Christmas. **14.** Mini vegetable/herb garden in pots, trays and hanging baskets, thrives in direct winter sunlight.

Top: Pots of African violets are combined in a basket of fern and Chinese evergreen. Bottom: The ancient art of bonsai can take many forms. The relatively young juniper pictured above is trained in the bonsai style.

The best way to find out what your light conditions are is to note how much direct sun penetrates a room and measure it in footcandles (see page 44). Check each room—you will be surprised at how much light some rooms have and how dim others are. Repeat this process every two months and more often where light is marginal. The more northern latitudes will register the most change between summer and winter. This light inventory, judiciously followed, will keep you in step with the changing seasons.

Plant Mobility

Like wine, some plants travel better than others. Weeping figs (*Ficus benjamina* 'Exotica') and gardenias, for example, are very sensitive to changes in position—they can easily lose all of their leaves upon being moved. It takes them awhile to recuperate from the shock of moving before "coming back" with new leaves.

When bringing a plant into your home from the nursery, be particularly watchful of its reaction. Wilting may be due to a drastic change in the environment, such as from a very humid condition or from a vastly different light. Water it unless the potting mix already feels moist. (Overwatering can produce symptoms identical to dehydration wilt.) Even more important at this time is to increase humidity to reduce further loss of moisture. (See page 25.) Be sure to check the foliage (and flowers, if any) to determine that the wilt is not caused by an infestation of some parasite, such as aphids, mites or white fly. Start the new plant off in a location that has the brightest possible indirect light. (Never put a plant in direct sunlight when it is wilted.) Some plants, such as coleus, piggyback and *Campanula*, will droop the moment they feel too thirsty. Try to avoid this wilting because it reduces a plant's vitality.

Keep plants away from cold or hot air currents. Misting the atmosphere around the plant is a temporary measure at best, and the leaves of some plants (such as the African violet) should not be misted at all. Increase humidity by other means. Keep soil evenly moist and do not feed the new plant for the first month. After a few weeks, you can move it to an area that has the light recommended for that species. Symptoms of poor light are not usually evident immediately; but some plants, such as asparagus ferns, will register their complaint about inadequate light within a week to 10 days. Their fernlike foliage begins to yellow and then to fall.

Mobilize your Indoor Garden

In creating a dramatic effect, remember that it takes less time to move large specimens than a host of small potted plants. An environmental inventory may lead to a plant redecorating scheme—because you may have to move some plants, why not go all the way and develop a seasonal spot for each plant? See the example for redecorating by the season on page 19.

Right: *Tolmeia menziesii* is the popular piggyback plant, so called because of its unusual leaves, which grow one on top of the other.

Make it easy to move plants as the seasons and lighting conditions change. Here are some ways:

Pots are the most obvious containers designed for easy movement. They are lightweight and come in sizes small enough to put almost anywhere—on tables and sideboards or in bookcases. See page 22.

Wooden platforms on casters with a detachable tote rope provide an easy way to move large plants that can't be picked up. They can be moved as the season dictates. The platform also keeps terra-cotta saucers off of the floor. Casters may also be mounted directly onto decorative wooden boxes so that they can be moved around effortlessly.

Plant perambulators or carts loaded with plants can make a permanent display in the living room—permanent, that is, until the sun changes with the season and it is time to perambulate into the dining room to recapture the afternoon sun. Carts can be constructed to blend in with any decor—fine wood veneers or chrome and glass can make a plant cart welcome in any room.

Pulleys allow great mobility—vertically. They make it possible to move plants up into the sun's direct rays in the summer and back down again in the winter. In a skylight, the reverse is possible—plants that would fry in the collected heat of a skylight in the summer can be lowered into the cool of the room via pulley. If several plant pulleys are mounted together, you can change the composition of plant groupings as the mood strikes. With pulleys your ivy, heart leaved philodendron or wandering Jew can be raised as they grow down toward the floor.

Brackets. Plants mounted on swinging brackets can be moved into or out of direct sunlight as the day or season progresses. These brackets are traditionally made from cast iron, and can be mounted on a window frame to give plants an easy environmental change. Plants can even be swung out of an open window to get a breath of fresh air.

The Year-round Garden

"Stage manage" a year-round plant show. Foliage plants can act as the supporting cast for the flowering showoffs. Bring outdoor plants indoors for short periods—use a handtruck to move large trees in 2-foot boxes. Bonsai and other small plants in decorative containers can be used as table centerpieces at dinner parties. Rhododendrons and other outdoor flowering plants can be grouped indoors for several days without harm—try this for a dramatic effect the next time you give a party. Potted annuals and perennials can be grown on the "south forty" and brought indoors at the height of their bloom to beautify a dining room. These visiting star performers will add seasonal color and interest to your indoor garden.

This is the greenhouse area off of the front entrance to the house featured on pages 16-17. The plants are undergoing special care, along with newly propagated species.

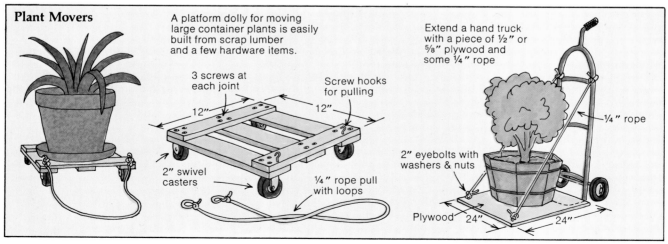

Plant Movers

A platform dolly for moving large container plants is easily built from scrap lumber and a few hardware items.

3 screws at each joint

12"   12"

Screw hooks for pulling

2" swivel casters

¼" rope pull with loops

Extend a hand truck with a piece of ½" or ⅝" plywood and some ¼" rope

¼" rope

2" eyebolts with washers & nuts

Plywood   24"   24"

HOUSEPLANT BASICS

The fundamentals of growing houseplants include knowing light, soil, moisture, food and temperature requirements.

The single most important thing to remember about any houseplant is this: The roots of the plant are confined to the container. They cannot search deeper or wider for sustenance. The plant depends on you for food and water the same as a pet dog. Fortunately plants do not have to be walked. In the following pages, you will find explicit directions for growing plants in containers. There are sections on light, temperature, humidity, soil, water, feeding, handling dormancy, potting and repotting, pruning and grooming, plus a section on problems and how to solve them.

Selecting Plant Containers

Pots and other containers suitable for plants are all around us. You can spend a fortune on a piece of imported china in which to show off your finest fern or flowering plant, but you can also spend nothing and have a fine container. For example, you can start seeds and cuttings in the bottom third of a milk carton or in a plastic margarine dish. In between these extremes is every imaginable kind of container for indoor or outdoor use, either for resting on surfaces or for hanging.

Clay Pots. These traditional containers are hard to beat. They range in size from 2 to 18 or more inches in diameter and until recently they have been readily available with saucers to fit. But the present enthusiasm for gardening has created such a shortage that saucers are sometimes scarce. So don't throw away a good clay saucer, or pot for that matter.

Before you place a plant into a clay pot, soak the pot in a pail or basin of water —preferably for several hours. Otherwise, the thirsty, dry clay will rob needed moisture from the soil and roots of your plant. When you have the time, scrub used clay pots with a stiff brush and warm water to get rid of residue dirt and possible carry-over diseases. You can also run them through a dishwasher.

A word of caution. Moisture seeps through clay saucers. In time moisture will mar wood and rot carpeting. A round of half-inch cork cut to fit under a saucer will dissipate the moisture. Plastic and glazed ceramic saucers do not present this problem.

Glazed Pots. Plant containers can be very decorative, especially for indoor plants. Many of these cachepots have a distinctly oriental feeling that adapts surprisingly well to almost any kind of decor. Many nurseries and garden centers now stock an array of glazed pots and trays for bonsai, which can also be used for other plants or for miniature landscapes. If you select a container that does not have a drainage hole, the best practice is to grow the plant in a slightly smaller clay or plastic pot that has drainage holes, and slip it inside the more decorative container. To camouflage the edges of the utilitarian pot, carpet the surface with florist's sheet moss, water polished stones or small shells.

Plastic Pots. Plastic containers have the distinct advantage of being light-

The variety in hanging plants is infinite. Pictured here is the colorful and easy-to-grow nasturtium.

weight. They are generally less expensive than clay and come in the same range of sizes. On a limited budget you can achieve a good-looking effect simply by using all white plastic pots. The ones in bright colors tend to look garish unless a color scheme is worked out with care. Plastic pots made to simulate terra cotta are probably the most attractive, especially for hanging baskets.

Wooden Boxes or Planters. Wooden planters made of rot-resistant redwood or cypress look attractive and also last a long time. Unfortunately, the commercial product is seldom well designed and all too often is held together by metal banding that rusts quickly. The best way is to build (or have built) your own wooden planter boxes, designed to fit your particular needs. Don't overlook marine plywood as a relatively inexpensive material from which to construct planters. Plans for building your own containers are available from California Redwood and American Plywood. See page 140.

Baskets. Many kinds of baskets make striking holders for plants, but they will rot quickly when subjected to constant moisture. If a basket is purely for show, to hide a utilitarian pot, be sure to place a saucer inside to collect excess water. If you wish to plant flowers, herbs or vegetables directly in a basket, line it first with heavy-duty polyethylene plastic. Since baskets do not tend to be strong containers, it is a good idea to fill them with a lightweight soilless medium.

Hanging Baskets. Hanging "baskets" can actually be made out of clay, plastic, pottery, wire, or reeds. A slightly larger woven basket or decorative pot can always hide a plain pot. And there are many interesting hangers in retail shops. You might like to macramé one from string or yarn, or fashion one out of metal or plastic.

Meeting Light Requirements

Photosynthesis, the process by which plants grow, is triggered by light. Plants vary in the amount of light they need, but most perform satisfactorily in a fairly wide range of intensities. Four basic light categories apply to indoor gardens:

The specimen *Ficus benjamina* forms a canopy over a day bed in this New York City apartment with good light. The humidity from the moist pebble tray on the radiator is good for all the plants in the room.

☐ *sunny* areas receive at least 5 hours of direct sunlight in winter. Usually a window facing southeast, south or southwest admits this amount of light;

☐ *semisunny* locations receive 2 to 5 hours of sun each day in winter. East or west windows are in this category;

☐ *semishady* places have bright, open light, but little or no direct sunlight;

☐ *shady* areas receive no sunlight, but have enough light to cast a shadow.

How much light you have. Many things affect how much light comes into your windows. The part of the world in which you live is important. For example, in the Rocky Mountains sunlight in winter is much more intense than in New England. Smoke from local industry may make sunny days hazy. Trees and shrubs will cut down on light—they can make a southern, eastern or western window suitable for shade-loving plants. A white house next door or a cement driveway will reflect light. Clean windows also mean more light. And don't forget—window screens reduce light by as much as 30 percent.

Day length affects plants. When days are longest, plants will do noticeably better in your house. Windows that face east and west will be sunny, while south-facing locations will need to be curtained to limit sun.

The length of day also determines when certain plants bloom. Poinsettias and Christmas cacti set flower buds in autumn when days begin to shorten. Calceolarias and tuberous begonias set buds when days become longer.

Artificial Light

Fluorescent lights make it possible for your plants to thrive in the places where you'll enjoy them most. Even your basement or attic can become a veritable greenhouse filled with beautiful flowers. Little money is needed to change a dimly lit spot into an attractive display of healthy plants.

Plants growing under fluorescent light don't have to cope with long periods of cloudy weather. Light intensity is the same in December as it is in June (provided tubes are replaced once every 6 to 12 months). Fluorescent light is cool; it never burns tender foliage. (See pages 62-73 for more information.)

The Air Surrounding Your Plants

Fresh, moist air helps plants thrive indoors. But it is unusual for a home to have prolonged temperatures below 68°F or to have relative humidity above 50 percent.

Humidity. Excessive dryness in a home is not only harmful to plants, but also can damage furniture and make the inhabitants uncomfortable. A cool vapor humidifier is an excellent way to increase humidity. Portable units can be placed where needed. Also you may want to have a humidifier installed as a part of your home's central heating system. Some are fairly inexpensive and well worth the cost for its effects on the plants, as well as on you.

Other ways to increase humidity are to group plants and to set the pots on trays of moist vermiculite, perlite or pebbles. Frequent misting helps humidity loving plants get moisture from the air and cleans the leaves for better breathing as well. If spraying will harm floors, walls or furniture, keep a large sheet of plastic or a drop cloth handy to cover what is necessary during spraying.

Temperature. Most plants will grow in a temperature range of 65° to 75°F. A few degrees above or below these figures shouldn't be harmful. Plants from the tropics suffer when the temperature goes below 60°. On the other hand, plants such as cinerarias and camellias do best with a maximum temperature of 65°. Such cool-loving plants would like a sun porch that is cool but does not freeze in winter.

Where winters are severe, a tender plant placed close to the window pane may freeze. At night, put a piece of cardboard between the plant and the window, or move it to a warmer part of the room. Be sure to keep plants out of direct drafts of hot or cold air.

A photographer's tripod sheds more light on plants when needed, and can be folded up and stored away when company comes.

Good Earth for Containers

Unless you have a place in which to prepare potting soils, time to do the work, and an easy way to obtain ingredients, it is a good idea to buy potting soils that are already mixed. On the other hand, potting mixtures are easy to make. Preparing soils yourself makes it possible to try different recipes for different types of plants. The following list contains descriptions of several basic soil mixtures that meet the needs of most plants.

A good all-purpose potting soil can be made by mixing together 2 parts garden soil, 1 part leaf mold and 1 part sand. This suits plants like geraniums, amaryllis, dracaenas, palms and oxalis.

High humus content is important for such plants as African violets, begonias, philodendrons and azaleas. They do well in a mixture of equal parts sand, peat moss, garden soil and leaf mold.

Plants from the desert need a gritty, lean-growing medium. Most cacti and other succulents will flourish in a mixture of 1 part garden soil, 1 part sand, ½ part decayed leaf mold and ½ part crushed clay flowerpot or brick. To each ½ bushel of this mixture, add a cup each of ground horticultural limestone and bone meal. Mixture should drain rapidly.

Air plants, called epiphytes, are cultivated in such mediums as osmunda fiber, unshredded sphagnum moss and chipped redwood bark. Most orchids and bromeliads are classed as epiphytes.

Take advantage of soil substitutes. Horticultural perlite is as light as a feather and makes a perfect substitute for sand. Vermiculite, in place of leaf mold, will lighten and condition heavy, sticky soil and make it acceptable to plants that need a well-aerated soil. These inexpensive soil substitutes are already sterilized, and can be purchased in small quantities at garden centers.

What growing "soilless" means. Soilless growing mediums are popular for container gardening. Perfected at Cornell University and the University of California, both formulas are similar. The main difference is that the Cornell mix uses vermiculite instead of the fine sand used by UC. The Cornell formula can be bought under such trade names as Jiffy Mix, Pro Mix and Redi-Earth. The UC formula is available under the names First Step and Super Soil.

Prepackaged basic soilless mixes are available from your garden center under many trade names. Based on Cornell University and University of California studies, they have been formulated for all types of houseplants.
Shown left to right: mix with high humus content for plants such as African violets, an all-purpose mix for most houseplants, a formula suited to terrariums, and a gritty lean-growing medium for cacti and other succulents. The mixes are composed of various kinds and amounts of ingredients discussed in the text.

To increase humidity, group plants together on a large pot saucer or metal tray filled with pebbles. Keep water in the container just to the top of the pebbles. Don't allow pot bottoms to rest in the water. A few chips of charcoal will keep the water sweet.

Whether you water plants from above or allow them to soak up water from below, make sure the watering is thorough. Most people agree that watering from above is easier. After a few minutes, pour off any excess water that accumulates in the saucer. To retain moisture in a decorative pot, place a utilitarian pot inside it and layer it with florist's sheet moss, as shown.

If you want to mix your own soilless growing medium, here is a recipe for the Cornell mix:

4 quarts #2 grade vermiculite	2 tablespoons limestone
4 quarts shredded peat moss	4 tablespoons dried cow manure
1 level tablespoon superphosphate	or steamed bone meal

Do your mixing in a large plastic pail. Be sure it is clean and dry before adding the ingredients. Select a pail that has a tight-fitting lid; it will keep insects out and also allow you to keep the medium moist, always ready for potting.

The soilless mediums are not only sterile and therefore conducive to healthy root growth, free of pests and disease, but they are also lightweight. This is especially important where large containers are involved, in rooftop gardening, and for hanging basket plantings.

How and When to Water

Common sense is your most valuable guide in knowing when a potted plant needs to be watered. Most roots like to grow in a medium that is moist—not dripping or oozing with water, not dusty dry. When it is time to add more water, the soil will have begun to dry out, and after watering it will be wet for a few hours. If you let a plant wilt before becoming moist again, you have waited too long to water. Dip sticks and moisture-sensitive paper are marketed to help you determine when it is time to water.

Constant saturation is good for a few plants. These include *Acorus*, bamboo, calla lily, Chinese evergreen and *Cyperus*.

Desert plants (most cacti and other succulents) need a period of dryness in-between the times they are moist. However, drought-loving plants grown in pots need to be watered more frequently than they would receive rain in their natural habitat; potted plants dry out more rapidly than in the open ground.

To water or not to water. You can determine whether a plant needs to have water applied to its roots in at least two ways. Insert a finger about an inch into the soil to feel whether it is moist. Rub a bit of the surface layer of soil between your thumb and index finger. If the soil is like dry powder, watering is needed. If your fingers get coated with water or mud, do not add water. If the soil you touch has a pleasing dampness, chances are good that watering won't be necessary for another 24 hours, possibly longer. Wilted foliage also usually signals a need for more moisture. Conversely, it may mean that you have watered too much and that the plant's roots have rotted.

A severely dried out plant, such as this coleus, can be immersed in a pail of water to the pot rim. Wait until top soil is well moistened, then drain and return to its growing spot. After a short time, it will return to its original healthy looking state.

The time honored test of when to water is to insert a finger about 1 inch below the soil surface. If it is dry, it is time to water.

Inexpensive plastic hand sprayers can increase the humidity with frequent mistings of water. Pressurized models are also available.

How often to water. Plants need varying amounts of water, depending on the season, the sizes and kinds of containers and the plants themselves.

Seasons. When days are short, cloudy and humid, plants use less water than when days are long, clear and sunny. If temperatures can be kept favorable, and fertilizing is constant, plants grown under fluorescent lights do as well in autumn and winter as in spring.

Sizes and kinds of containers have much to do with how often plants need moisture. If the pot is small, watering may be a daily requirement. Some plants need small pots. However, if you can't keep a plant moist, it probably needs re-potting. Clay pots allow moisture to evaporate through the walls, while glazed and plastic kinds transpire moisture only through the soil surface. Therefore, plants potted in clay need more water than those planted in glazed or plastic pots.

Basic watering rules. Be thorough. Usually it is easier and faster to water container-grown plants from above. It takes more time to submerge a pot in water to its rim, a procedure called bottom watering, but it is good for plants that have dried out severely, as well as for those you buy already in full bloom from a florist. Bottom watering is also the best way to water plants growing on slabs of tree fern trunk and hanging baskets made of this material. Allow to drain, then return to growing space.

Whether you add moisture from above or below, pot saucers must have excess water poured off within an hour after watering to discourage rot-causing organisms from attacking roots.

Water for indoor gardening. If you can drink the water where you live, then it is safe for potted plants. How you use the water is far more vital to plant life than the chemical content.

Softened water may be harmful. Zeolitic water softeners can injure plants. This kind of softener replaces the calcium in water with sodium, which does not settle out or evaporate. The sodium will accumulate in houseplant soil to a harmful extent. If you have a water softener, install a tap in the water line before the water reaches the softener, so that you can provide unsoftened water for your plants.

Where water is alkaline. In parts of the country where the soil is alkaline and the water is hard, it is difficult to grow acid-loving plants. Generous use of acidic peat moss and acid-reacting fertilizers will help offset the alkaline content in soil and water. Plants like azaleas, gardenias and camellias will benefit from regular applications of an iron chelate (ask at your garden center for a product that contains iron chelate) to keep the foliage a healthy dark green. When new foliage of these plants turns yellow, water with a solution of one ounce of iron sulfate in two gallons of water. Repeat treatment every other week until growth returns to its normal color.

Water temperature is important. Take the chill off of water before you use it on houseplants. Tropical plants are the most sensitive, but all may be harmed by having icy water applied either to roots or foliage. Water for houseplants should be barely warm or tepid—within 10°F of the room temperature.

How and When to Fertilize

Nitrogen, phosphates and potash are the three basic elements that plants need. When you pick up a container of houseplant fertilizer at your garden store, you will see a combination of figures, for example 12-6-6. These numbers always list in the same order the percentages of nitrogen, phosphates and potash. This fertilizer has 12 percent nitrogen, 6 percent phosphates and 6 percent potash.

Basics about fertilizing. Container plants need regular feeding when they are actively growing. Most houseplant fertilizers on the market have been formulated for use every two weeks. This is more effective than large monthly doses. Follow container directions for rate and frequency. Plants growing in synthetic soils need ⅛ to ½-strength fertilizer added every time they are watered.

People involved in all phases of container gardening—nursery owners, plant breeders, retailers and hobbyists—have favorite types of fertilizer. Some prefer dry formulas; some use only liquid fish emulsion; others use liquids for some plants and prefer dry types for others.

Many kinds of fertilizers are available: water soluble pellets, powders and liquids; dry tablets and sticks to insert in the soil; and time-release pellets. Whatever kind you choose, read the label first and follow the directions. Prevent root burn by always moistening the soil before adding fertilizer.

Too much fertilizer may cause leaf edges to turn brown in otherwise good growing conditions. Excess plant food may also cause lower leaves to drop prematurely, or the entire plant may wilt. If this happens to one of your plants, leach out the fertilizer by applying copious amounts of water, allow the soil to drain, then pour on more water. Or you can wash the old soil from the plant roots and repot into fresh soil.

Foliar feeding. In the tropics some jungle plants depend for nourishment on nitrogen from rain and on bird droppings washed down on them from overhanging trees. Read the labels at your garden store and you will find fertilizers that are specifically recommended for leaves. Apply every 2 to 4 weeks, according to directions. Foliar feeding should only supplement the fertilizers that are applied directly to the soil.

Following the fertilizer manufacturer's directions could have prevented the leaf burn caused from overfeeding this spider plant.

Rest and Recuperation

To some extent, nature's cycle for plant growth applies to those growing indoors the same as it does to those outdoors. Shorter days and cooler temperatures induce dormancy. Except for the length of day, centrally heated indoor environments offer plants a potentially endless summer. A constant environment is entirely possible in a fluorescent-lit garden where day length can be the same all year around. However, even artificially lit plants tend to have resting periods; growth slows and they need less food and water.

Tuberous and bulbous plants generally die to the ground while they rest. In cultivation we simply withhold food and water. However, not all bulbous plants die down. Potted *Agapanthus* and *Tulbaghia*, for example, stay leafy and green all year, sending up flowers after a time of active growth.

Tropical foliage plants are more conscious of warm, moist air than of seasonal periods of long and short days. Unless your home is unusually warm and humid in winter, plants like these will show a slowing of growth. Also, in these energy conscious days when many thermostats are being lowered a few degrees, most tropicals will slow down.

How to treat dormant plants. It is very important to the health of your potted plants that you realize when they are resting—or need a rest. Slowing down is most likely to occur after a flush of new growth or a period of heavy flowering. In the winter months, resting is especially typical of tropical plants that are kept where temperatures stay generally below 70°F.

Symptoms include absence of new growth, a tired appearance and yellow-

To remove the plant, tap the pot gently on the edge of the table, then examine the growing area. When roots fill the pot like this, the plant should be transplanted to a larger pot.

Below: A top-heavy *Peperomia* obviously needs a new pot. Gently tap it free from its container. Place a piece of broken pottery over the drainage hole in the new container. This keeps the soil from washing through the hole, thus clogging drainage. Put in some sterile potting medium, then the plant, and fill in with more soil. Firm with fingers to eliminate air pockets. Water well to moisten the soil thoroughly. Don't forget to soak clay pots before potting so that they will not rob moisture from the newly planted roots. Here we add stakes to support the tender stems. Use Twist-ems, yarn, or soft cloth strips. Wrap the tie gently around the stem, then tie it to the stake.

ing leaves that fall off. When these symptoms occur, apply less water than usual. Keep the soil just moist, never really wet. Do not apply any fertilizer. Cold, wet soil and feeding as if the weather is balmy kill countless houseplants during the winter. When a plant seems to be resting, do not repot it, but wait until the plant starts new leaf buds.

How and When to Pot

A container holds the private underworld of a plant. What goes on down there in the darkness may be a mystery, but it is vital to what you see above the soil. Pot size comes first. The best potting soil in the world will work at a disadvantage if it is contained in a pot that is too small or too large for the plant. The photos on these pages show how to pot and repot most types of plants.

A general rule about pot size is to use a pot whose diameter at the top equals $\frac{1}{3}$ to $\frac{1}{2}$ the height of the plant. This is illustrated in the repotting of the marigold on the next page. In most instances it is advisable to move a plant up to a pot only one size larger than the previous one. Although they are an exception, there are some plants which perform better when somewhat rootbound. Sago palms (*Cycas revoluta*) and the common garden geranium (*Pelargonium* species) are good examples of such plants; others are noted in the text of the encyclopedia section (pages 78–119).

Clean pots help to make gardening a pleasure. They also induce neat, orderly storage according to size. Before you use a pot that has been used before, scrub it clean. Plastic and glazed ones present no difficulty; treat them like dishes. To clean old, dirty clay pots, put them in a bucket and pour boiling water over them. Add $\frac{1}{2}$ cup of household bleach to the water and let stand for a few hours. After this soaking, it will be easy to scrub the pots so that they look like new. If you have an overabundance of any standard type of clay or plastic pot, give them to someone else you know who gardens.

Here, a straggly marigold is being repotted. To determine the proper size of the new pot, choose one with a diameter that is ⅓ the plant's height. Place some drainage material and soil in the pot, add the plant, and fill in with more soil. Pack down firmly with fingers. Soak in pail of water until thoroughly moistened. Trim off the old leaves and spent blooms and enjoy a healthier looking and happier plant.

Soil should be lightly moist for potting. If premixed soil is dry, add water to the bag, close tightly and knead thoroughly, as shown.

To repot a plant in a container without drainage, first remove the plant from its original container. Select the new one based on root size and the scale of the plant to container. Place a layer of broken pottery, small gravel or chips of charcoal in the bottom of the container. Add some sterile soil to the new pot. Loosen soil around roots of the plant. Place plant in position and add more soil to fill pot. Pack firmly with fingers to eliminate any air pockets, which can cause root damage. Remember not to fill the pot so full of soil that there is no room left for watering. Succulents should not be watered for a few days after transplanting. Clean the plant and pot and add a ground mulch such as sand or gravel if desired.

Good Grooming Techniques

Plants that grow in pots and other containers need regular trimming back in order to keep them attractively shaped and at a size that makes them pleasant to have around. There are two methods for shaping most plants: pinching and pruning.

Pinching. Pinching is a simple operation you do with your thumb and forefinger to remove the young tip growth of a stem that you want to branch out. For example, consider a young coleus plant. You have started it from seed or a cutting. If you let the plant grow without pinching, it will probably continue as one stem, going straight up and eventually becoming lanky and weak. So, as soon as possible, pinch out the growing tip. This causes dormant buds in the lower leaf axils to spring into active growth. Where you had 1 leader, there will now be 2. After 2 or 3 weeks, pinch the tips out of these 2 and you will then have a bushy plant of 4 stems, then 8 and finally 16 or more. Pinching is a handy thing to know about in gardening. It works especially well for soft-stemmed plants, such as wax and angel-wing begonias, young geraniums and coleus.

Pruning. Pruning is how you can keep more or less woody plants the right size and shape. You need a pair of small hand pruners to do this work. Plants such as Chinese hibiscus, bougainvillea, gardenia and jasmine need pruning to keep the branch framework well balanced and sturdy. After a flowering period, clip off long, weak branches that extend beyond the plant's overall shape.

Extras for a perfect container garden. Stakes, trellises and other means of supporting stems and branches will help you have a collection of beautiful plants.

Staking is an art practiced in most commercial greenhouses. Early in the life of such plants as chrysanthemum, tuberous begonias or poinsettias, each stem is tied to a dark green bamboo or wooden stake. This technique was used for the tall, leggy peperomia you see illustrated on page 30. You can train your plants in the same way in your container garden. Stake early—you can keep a straight stem straight, but you may not be able to uncrook a crooked one. Use pieces of soft yarn, strips of cloth or, better still, the commercially prepared Twist-ems to hold stems to stakes.

Totem poles are used to support some plants. They have various shapes, including the cylinder, cone and ball. Totem poles are usually cut out of osmunda fiber. They are ideal accessories for philodendron and episcia and for training English ivy to grow into unusual shapes.

Trellises certainly have a place in container gardening, although they are not seen frequently. You can put up a small wooden, wire or string trellis wherever you want a vine to climb. In a sunny window, 'Heavenly Blue' morning glories make a cheerful drapery of green and bright blue. The black-eyed Susan (*Thunbergia alata*) is another vine that will decorate a sunny window.

Topsoil should be kept raked and cleaned or covered with a layer of florist's sheet moss. You may also want to add bark mulching, polished stones or gravel for finishing touches.

Brown or yellow edges can keep a plant from looking its best. Some browning is normal with many tropicals that are grown indoors. Cut away the dried portion with sharp scissors, following the original shape of the leaves. The cleaned-up foliage makes the plant look more attractive and does not harm its health or growth.

Remove young tip growth from stems that you want to branch out. Simply pinch growth out with your thumb and forefinger. This keeps the plant bushy and compact.

Planting Hanging Baskets

Plants in hanging baskets are the trapeze artists of the plant world—they are at their best swinging, dangling or climbing. You can use pottery, wooden, wire or plastic hanging baskets (sold at garden centers and by mail). Regular clay and plastic flowerpots may be used also. The string, wire or chain used to hang them can hold a saucer in place so that water will not drip on the floor. The many kinds of decorative hangers can give a planter a style of its own.

Line wooden baskets with aluminum foil so that soil won't wash through cracks. Wire and plastic baskets need to be lined first with coarse, unmilled sphagnum moss or florist's sheet moss, then filled with soil. To prevent soil erosion some growers like to line the moss with burlap or add a saucer before putting in the soil and plant. (See photos and explanation.)

The culture of hanging basket plants varies according to the plant. In general they need evenly moist soil, good light, and average warmth (60 to 80°F). Water by immersing container at a sink or in a pail. Allow to soak, then drain long enough for the basket not to drip when it is rehung.

Good hanging basket plants that are easy to cultivate under average home conditions include:

Achimenes (Rainbow flower)
Basket begonias
Ceropegia woodii (Rosary vine)
Chlorophytum (Spider plant)
Cissus
Epipremnum aureum
Episcia
Ficus pumila (Creeping fig)
Hoya (Wax plant)
Kalanchoe manginii

Mahernia verticillata (Honey bell)
Pellionia
Philodendron micans
Pilea depressa
Plectranthus australis
Sedum morganianum (Donkey's tail)
Sedum dasyphyllum
Senecio rowleyanus
Soleirolia soleirolii (Baby's tears)
Wandering Jew

To fill a hanging wire basket, stuff the frame with moist sphagnum moss. Add another lining of burlap, if desired. Place a saucer (an aluminum pie tin is perfect) in the bottom to keep soil from eroding. Follow the usual potting procedures. Then attach hangers and immerse the basket in a large pail of water to moisten thoroughly. Half-round wire frames are available for attaching to flat surfaces. Plant wooden baskets in the same way, except use foil or plastic to keep the soil from washing through.

Orchids are among the most spectacular of all blooming houseplants. Above, an orchid collector selects species that bloom throughout the year.

Setting the Stage

Indoor gardeners are a diverse group ranging from the kindergarten enthusiast who first sprouts a bean seed, to the retired professional who has mastered the art of orchid hybridization. Even people who are not ambulatory can enjoy miniature gardening at their bedside.

You are an indoor gardener even if you possess only one plant—perhaps a living gift from a special occasion or a coleus cutting that you have nurtured along. Your "garden" may be the kitchen windowsill, a fluorescent-lit bookcase or a shelf or desk where you work.

Indoor gardeners do not "grow" plants—the plants grow themselves. Your responsibility is to provide the proper *environment* in which plants can flourish. Unlike outdoor plants, which send out roots in search of water or food, indoor plants are confined to containers and depend on the gardener to supplement Mother Nature.

However, even with the best of care, we must be prepared to accept the inevitable: Like all living things, plants eventually die and must be replaced.

Help for the Indoor Gardener

Everywhere we look today plants are being sold: in plant shops and boutiques; in department stores, nurseries and flower shops; even in supermarkets and hardware stores. Indoor plants and gardening supplies have become "big business" as more and more people have discovered the excitement and challenge of indoor gardening. To meet the demand, countless new products have come on the market. Among this array of gadgets, accessories and devices are quite a few helpful items for indoor gardening. The photo on page 23 shows just a few examples of what is available, taken from a random sampling of retail outlets. Analyze your own gardening needs, tastes and desires as much as possible before visiting your local gardening outlet. Such forethought helps you in selecting just the items that you will find really useful in your container garden.

Home Environmental Inventory

Unlike the house shown on pages 16-17, few interiors offer ideal gardening facilities. Most homes, shops or offices are too hot and dry for most plants and have too little or sometimes even too much sun. Take a look at your space from the plant's point of view. First, consider the light. Can you meet the plant's light requirement by either natural or artificial means? Use the chart on pages 128-138 as a guide. Reputable nurseries and plant shops can also help you make an educated selection after you have selected a plant site.

Second, pay attention to the amount of humidity. Where are the best places to locate plants so that they will receive needed moisture from the air? Kitchens and bathrooms with their steam and running water are obvious spots. But kitchens also have ovens and burners that give off excessive heat and use up moisture in the air. This frequent heating and drying action can offset the advantages of running water. Place a thermometer where you wish to place a plant. Check it when your stove is getting maximum use. Misting the air can minimize the effects of a high temperature by replacing the moisture lost through heating. And don't forget that humidity is needed in other rooms as well. Some plants, however, such as the cactus, prefer dry locations.

The third, often neglected, consideration in locating plants is design. Where will a plant look the best? How does it relate to the architectural structure and interior decor? In planning your interior "horticultural design," apply the same principles you would use in arranging furniture or works of art. For some, the desire to grow plants indoors becomes so strong that all level surfaces are soon covered with a variety of growing things. Such a situation is pictured in the photograph opposite, which some might consider "cluttered" while others would say "delightful." The current trend in decorating with plants favors fewer and larger plants, but don't let that stop you if a multitude of plants is

This extensive indoor container garden requires considerable maintenance, but rewards the owner with varied foliage and exciting blooms.

what pleases you: Some people like a single specimen plant, while others want an entire collection, but collections can require a lot of upkeep.

Interior spaces have many "microclimates," just like a backyard garden. There are hot spots, shady nooks and damaging drafts, along with perfect growing spots. Seek out those places where plants will thrive. Don't be afraid to try plants in many places. Experimental, adventurous gardeners sometimes violate ironclad rules and restrictions with success. We know of some who have moved bamboo, oleander, dwarf citrus, and Japanese maples indoors and grown them there for many years. The secret is knowing the particular climate of a room and responding to the individual requirements of particular plants. One gardener reported that her piggyback is only happy on top of the refrigerator and she has to lift its leaves up whenever she wants to open the freezer door. But she feels that the reward of a beautiful, thriving plant is worth this inconvenience.

The Indoor Potting Shed

When your house is also your garden, one major problem is where to do all those simple but messy chores. You can't repot without handling soil and this kind of operation can be a problem in the living room, kitchen, or almost any indoor space, for that matter. In the process of gathering information and photographing indoor gardens for this book, we ran across several inventive people who had solved the problems of gardening indoors. Several suggestions are offered on the following pages for creating a workspace that will confine your garden chores to a convenient area. Because we have seen them in use we know these designs are functional.

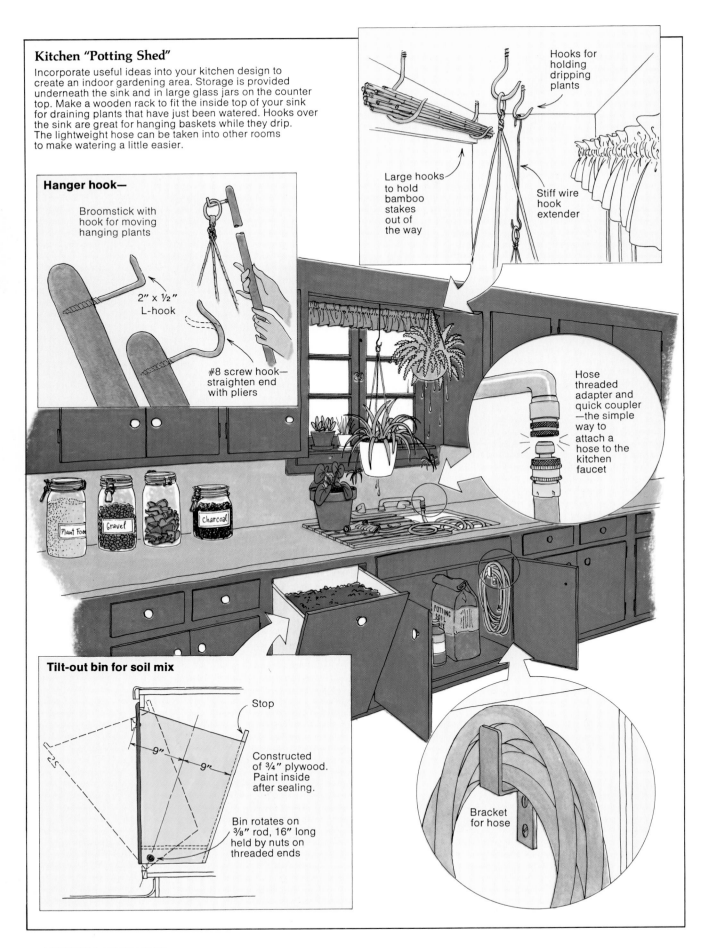

Kitchen "Potting Shed"

Incorporate useful ideas into your kitchen design to create an indoor gardening area. Storage is provided underneath the sink and in large glass jars on the counter top. Make a wooden rack to fit the inside top of your sink for draining plants that have just been watered. Hooks over the sink are great for hanging baskets while they drip. The lightweight hose can be taken into other rooms to make watering a little easier.

Hooks for holding dripping plants

Large hooks to hold bamboo stakes out of the way

Stiff wire hook extender

Hanger hook—

Broomstick with hook for moving hanging plants

2" x ½" L-hook

#8 screw hook— straighten end with pliers

Plant Food

Gravel

Charcoal

Hose threaded adapter and quick coupler —the simple way to attach a hose to the kitchen faucet

POTTING SOIL

Tilt-out bin for soil mix

Stop

9"

9"

Constructed of ¾" plywood. Paint inside after sealing.

Bin rotates on ⅜" rod, 16" long held by nuts on threaded ends

Bracket for hose

Closet Garden Workshop

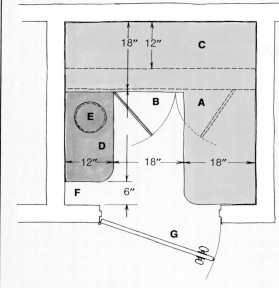

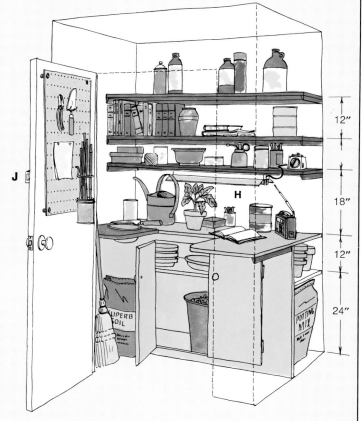

Here are two ideas for turning a spare closet—walk-in or standard—into an indoor gardening area. Both provide ample storage for tools, pots and garden products and offer a retreat for all those messy gardening chores that can be shut away from the rest of the house. Provide plastic drop cloths for catching spilled soil, water, or leaves. Plant growth lights on automatic timers allow you to leave problem plants inside during periods of recuperation. With careful planning you can utilize every inch of the area, even the back of the closet door.

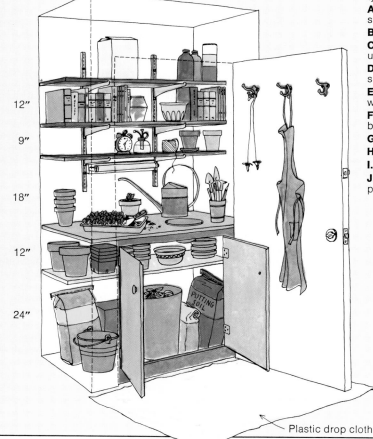

Plastic drop cloth

Key to floor plans of walk-in (above) and standard type closet (below):

A. ¾-inch plywood work counter with plasticized surface (e.g. 'Formica').

B. Storage cabinet underneath counter for storage.

C. ¾-inch plywood shelves over counter and in cabinet underneath counter for storage.

D. ¾-inch plywood work counter with oil base painted surface, butcher block, or plasticized surface.

E. 8-inch plastic bowl set into counter to catch excess water and soil.

F. Corner storage for long-handled tools such as mops, brooms and plant light on tripod.

G. Pegboard with hooks for tools.

H. Plant growth lights on automatic timer.

I. Hooks for extra tools, hangers, aprons, etc.

J. Lock to keep children and pets away from garden products.

Houseplant Problems

The chart on the opposite page offers advice for specific houseplant problems. You should realize, though, that the exact cause of a particular problem is not always an easy thing to determine. A plant doctor or nursery clerk usually has to ask the owner of an ailing plant many questions before making an accurate diagnosis. Indoor gardeners should get into the habit of asking themselves the same questions an expert would before seeking outside help. Such questions include: How often do you water the plant? Where is the plant located? Have you recently moved the plant to a new location? Do you fertilize the plant regularly? When was the last time you fertilized, and what product did you use? Did you follow the suggested dilution rates? Have you sprayed the plant with insecticide? Which product did you use?

The answers to these questions, combined with the advice in the chart on the next page and the information found in the Plant Selection Guide (page 128) should solve many problems. For example, your *Philodendron* has leaves that are limp and yellowish, and the overall vigor of the plant is poor. By comparing the answers to the questions asked above to the information in the Plant Selection Guide, you may discover that you have not been watering the plant enough and have forgotten to fertilize it on a monthly basis.

The most common houseplant problems are related to too much or too little water, too much or too little fertilizer, not using the appropriate potting medium or placing the plant in the wrong environment.

Occasionally a houseplant is attacked by an insect or fungus, which makes it important to determine from the beginning whether the problem is cultural (too much sun, water, wrong soil mix, etc.) or caused by pest or disease. More often than not, if insects are doing the damage, they will be visible to the naked eye or with the aid of a small magnifying glass.

Descriptions of the most common houseplant pests can be found in the chart on the opposite page, along with the recommended solutions. It is rare for houseplants to be attacked by a fungus. The problem can usually be improved by moving the plants to a less humid, brighter location, or by applying a commercial fungicide.

Commercial products for houseplant problems fall into several categories. Insecticides control insect pests, while miticides are special formulations for the control of mites and related life; both are included in the more general term pesticides. Fungicides eradicate fungus diseases and any of these may be formulated as a systemic product which works by actually being absorbed into the plant through the roots or leaves. Herbicides kill plants and when properly applied can be used for the control of weeds. Once you determine what the pest is, ask for an appropriate product, one which lists the specific pest and/or host plant on the label.

Several manufacturers have made prediluted pesticide products that are available in aerosol cans or pump sprays. These products make good sense for the indoor gardener, especially when the amount needed is minimal. Be sure to read and follow all label directions carefully. Don't try to outsmart the manufacturer when it comes to application rates and precautions. And when applying an aerosol product, be sure to keep the can at least 18 inches away from the leaf to avoid leaf damage.

Plant or Insect	Problem	Solution
Clusters of tiny bugs on new growth. Foliage is malformed and discolored.	Aphids.	Eradicate with pesticide such as Malathion used as directed.
Leaf edges crisp and brown; quick withering of new growth.	Too much heat. Lack of humidity. Uneven soil moisture.	Lower temperature. Increase humidity. Avoid severely dry soil, then flooding.
Yellow lower leaves, some dropping off.	Improper growing conditions or age.	Avoid temperature extremes. Increase humidity. Give fresh air. Keep soil evenly moist. May need biweekly feeding. Be sure there are no gas leaks. After these precautions are taken, yellow leaf probably means the plant is dying and should be removed.
Nearly transparent spots on leaves caused by sucking of plant juices. Fine webs on underside of leaves. Look for tiny insects with magnifying glass.	Mites (Use magnifying glass or look for webs.)	Spray firm-leaved plants with forceful stream of water. Use an aerosol spray that indicates use against red spider mites.
Soft, slimy slugs on leaves or shell-covered snails around plants. Silvery streaks on foliage.	Slugs and snails.	Constant vigilance in plant sanitation. Use commercial slug bait.
Leaves appear lifeless; frequent wilting; requires daily watering.	Temperature too high; pot too small.	Put in cooler location. Change to larger container. Provide more sunlight or fluorescent light.
Plants that should bloom do not produce flowers.	Lack of moisture or sunlight. Too much fertilizer.	Increase humidity. Keep evenly moist. Feed less; don't use high nitrogen fertilizer during blooming season.
Flower buds drop off before opening.	Improper growing conditions.	Avoid high or fluctuating temperatures. Be sure plant is out of drafts. Provide more humidity; mist twice daily.
Soft powder-covered insects look like specks of cotton on a plant.	Mealybugs.	If only a few, touch with cotton swabs dipped in alcohol. Sprays containing Malathion eliminate large colonies.
Soft or hard scales, brown or black, round, slow-moving insects.	Scale.	Small infestations on glossy-leaved plants can be removed by washing with strong soapsuds, or spray with aerosol pesticide recommended for eliminating these slow-moving insects.
Yellowish brown, sometimes silvery, spots on leaves.	Too much sun.	Give more shade.
White or yellowish rings and spots on foliage.	Cold water on leaves and roots.	Always use water at room temperature. Don't let hot sun shine on foliage that has drops of water on it.

USING NATURAL LIGHT

Make the most of your natural light, learn how to measure it and how it affects your plants.

Houseplants come to us from all over the tropical and subtropical world. Most of the plants that we grow in our homes are from the cool tropics. Those from the warm tropics require greenhouse culture. The tropical belt has a tremendous variety of lighting conditions, from the dimly lit understory of dense jungles to the strong sunlight of the savannas (grasslands with few trees and seasonal rains). Plants differ in their light-intensity and light-duration needs. When a plant is transported from its native habitat to an indoor environment, these differences must be respected, or the plant will not thrive.

Some plants are extremely sensitive and just seem to resist any change. When you move them from the nursery to your home or from one room to another, they may temporarily wilt or drop their leaves.

The Light Spectrum

Light is an essential part of the recipe for healthy plant life. A general understanding of its nature as it relates to indoor gardening will help to keep the cymbidium in bloom and the fiddleleaf fig from getting sunburned leaves.

Light is radiant energy. Technically, it is the visible portion of the electromagnetic wavelength spectrum. This spectrum is composed of rays of varying wavelengths and frequencies. In addition to visible light it contains invisible solar radiations, such as X rays, radio and TV waves, and shortwaves. Heat is the result of energy at the short wave length end of the visible spectrum. This increasing natural light level also means an increase in temperature. As a corollary of this, temperatures can be reduced by filtering light through curtains.

Visible "white" sunlight is actually a blend of red, orange, yellow, green, blue, and violet rays—all the rainbow hues seen in a child's glass prism. Beyond the visible blue-violet rays at one end of the spectrum are invisible ultraviolet rays; at the other end, invisible infrared rays lie just beyond the visible red rays.

The rays that make up white light affect plants differently. The blue and violet rays promote foliage growth. Plants grown under blue light tend to be compact and have lush, dark green leaves, but few flowers. As far as we know, neither yellow nor green rays affects plant growth in any major way. Red and far-red light encourage flowering, along with the elongation and expansion of various plant parts. Although plant scientists have been able to identify these effects, they have yet to discover how they occur.

The United States Department of Agriculture Experimental Station in Beltsville, Maryland is researching the relationship of light quality to plant life. This work has made possible the development of special "growth lamps" which are discussed in the chapter on artificial lighting. The so-called "growth lamps" provide nearly all of the wavelengths that occur in natural daylight and represent a real breakthrough for indoor gardening. Several manufacturers now produce "growth lamps" (see pages 62-73).

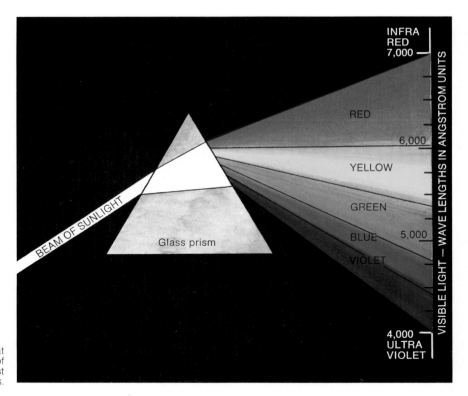

A prism allows us to see the color waves that comprise light: waves at the extreme ends of the color spectrum are the ones most important to plants.

How Light Affects Plants

Some plants are given too much light—particularly the ones from tropical rain forests. Many of them can't even tolerate filtered sunlight—they grow better in a sunless northern exposure than in a semishaded eastern one. When placed in the sun, their leaves may wilt during the hottest part of the day, curling downward and developing brown, burned spots. Some plants, such as the spider plant (*Chlorophytum*), will suffer outright leafburn if left in too much direct sun. The foliage may also change color in too much sunlight. Lush greens may bleach out to unhealthy yellows, a condition affecting *Schefflera*, *Philodendron*, ferns, and *Peperomia*.

No plant, regardless of its potential light tolerance, should be subjected to a drastic change of light without proper conditioning. (Good nurseries are now preconditioning their plants for home environments; you should ask if your plant has been acclimatized.) A plant that has been grown in shade can suffer fatal burning if moved abruptly to a sunny location. The results can be compared to a person, pale from winter indoor living, who goes to the beach and gets severely burned after spending only a few hours in the sun. A plant should be exposed to more light *gradually*, over a period of 3 to 4 weeks. More light should be introduced daily for increasingly longer periods, being watchful for any signs of damage. While some of the effects of too much sun can be offset by increased watering and humidity, the obvious solution is to move the plant into a more subdued light.

On the other hand, insufficient light will produce long, weak stems and leaves with less foliage than normal, as the plant stretches toward the light. Scientists call this extended stem growth *etiolation*. Low-light intensity will also inhibit plants from blooming. A plant surviving at the minimum illumination level only *maintains* itself; if it receives more light, it *grows*. Below minimum illumination, it *weakens* and may die. A plant in this state may appear healthy for some months, but, in fact, it is living off of stored carbohydrates and is slowly declining. It may not regain its vigor, even if it is again given adequate light.

Most flowering plants *require* direct light. They should be positioned so that they receive direct sunlight part of each day or supplemental artificial light if direct light is not possible. In the winter they can tolerate southern and western windowsill locations in most parts of the United States, and in summer can invariably take direct sun in eastern windows or late afternoon western ones.

Some plants produce more flowers if light intensity or duration is increased. African violets are a notable example: They will produce up to twice as many blooms if they have 16 hours of light rather than 8 hours, assuming a constant light intensity of 800 footcandles (see page 44). Most plants do well in more light than the optimum amount required, but few can tolerate less than their minimum requirement of light without serious consequences.

Light and Growth Interactions

Light regulates three major plant processes: photosynthesis, phototropism, and photoperiodism.

Photosynthesis. Light is life. It is one of the necessary ingredients for photosynthesis (photo = light, synthesis = to put together). It provides the energy required for the manufacture of a plant's food (and, in fact, is the basic source of all food energy, even for man). In the presence of light, water and atmospheric carbon dioxide are converted into carbohydrates. With these carbohydrates the plant produces new growth: foliage, roots, stems and blooms.

The presense of the right amount of light fosters luxuriant leaf growth and flowering. Photosynthesis stops with the absence of light. In the artificial atmosphere indoors, a plant's growing "season" can be greatly extended by the use of artificial light.

Phototropism. Phototropism is the effect of light on plant growth, causing the plant either to grow toward or away from the light source. Phototropism (photo = light, trope = to bend) is controlled by an auxin, or growth hormone, which occurs at the stem tips and in the youngest plant leaves. This auxin is highly reactive to light and causes the plant to adjust itself unceasingly to the light source. There are two kinds of phototropism. Positive tropism is the condition in which a plant moves toward the light source (the most common occurance); negative tropism occurs when a plant moves away from it.

Indoors, where light normally comes from windows, plants will bend toward them. To avoid developing permanently misshapen plants, rotate them occasionally to foster uniformly upright growth. Plants that grow rapidly need to be turned often.

This *Syngonium* is a victim of phototropism — it is forced to reach out for more light.

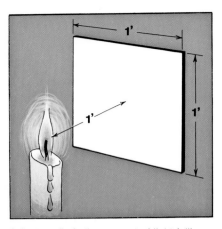

A footcandle is the amount of light falling on 1 square foot of surface located 1 foot away from 1 candle.

Artificial lighting should come from above—at least it should shine down on the top half of an erect plant. The best placement is directly overhead. Weeping plants, such as a hanging Boston fern, can be lit successfully from below, but the light must be more intense than when it shines from above the plant.

Photoperiodism. All plants are programmed to receive the amount of light present in their native enviroment; they also perform best in the rhythm of the light-darkness cycle found there. For many plants the length of night and day is a determining factor in the time required to reach maturity: that stage in a plant's life when reproduction (i.e. flowering) becomes possible.

Some plants flower best when the days are long—14 hours or more; these are called *long-day* plants. Some long-day plants are *Calceolaria*, tuberous begonia, cineraria, hibiscus, heather and nasturtium.

Conversely, other plants produce blooms when days are short; these are called *short-day* plants. Short-day plants will not form flower buds unless they receive at least 14 hours of darkness to set their flower buds, prior to blooming. Common short-day plants are gardenia, kalanchoe, chrysanthemum, Christmas cactus, poinsettia, cattleya orchids and bougainvillea.

Most plants, however, have no definite response—they are *day neutral.* They will bloom, generally on schedule, with either 8 or 16 hours of light daily. Bulbs are day neutral; tulips, daffodils and amaryllis all seem to perform well with differing day lengths.

Armed with the knowledge that 14 or more hours of light per day triggers flowering in long-day plants, indoor gardeners can force blooming any time of the year by using artificial light. On the other hand, many short-day plants, which require 12 or more hours of darkness to stimulate flowering, can be induced to bloom artificially by putting them into a dark closet at night and taking them out at noon, or by covering them with a photographer's black cloth or other light-shielding material.

The seasonal dormancy cycle for outdoor plants does not happen automatically for houseplants because the indoor enviroment does not have the periodic shifts in temperature and other natural impacts that outdoor plants must become accustomed to. Plants are healthiest when their natural habitats are duplicated, thereby encouraging natural stages of rest. Dormancy in woody plants can be induced by shortening the day and reducing watering. Although it seems like a lot of work to decrease the amount of light, water and feeding during a plant's "winter," most plants, even day-neutral ones, require a rest for healthy spring growth. Indeed, some flowering plants, such as gloxinia, *Ixia* and tuberous begonia, need a period of dormancy if they are to bloom at all.

Light Measurements

Light is measured either in footcandles or in lumens, depending on whether you are considering the object that is lighted or the source of the light.

Footcandles, f.c. for short, are the amount of light *received* on a surface. Lumens are the amount of light *emitted* by a light source.

Both natural sunlight and artificial light falling on a plant are measured in footcandles, while the light actually emitted by these sources rated in lumens.

One footcandle equals the amount of visible light that falls on one square foot of surface located one foot away from one candle. One lumen is the amount of light given off by one candle.

For example, a footcandle meter that is read at noon on a clear summer day may register 10,000 f.c., while a reading at the same time on an overcast winter day may be as low as 500 f.c.

Light readings inside are much lower than outside. The direct sun entering a window on a clear summer afternoon may register 4,000 to 8,000 footcandles, while in the shade at the side of the window the meter may only indicate 600 f.c. At the same time and on the same day, it may show only 150 to 250 f.c. at the window receiving indirect sun.

Lamps are rated in lumens. A 40-watt, rapid-start fluorescent tube initially

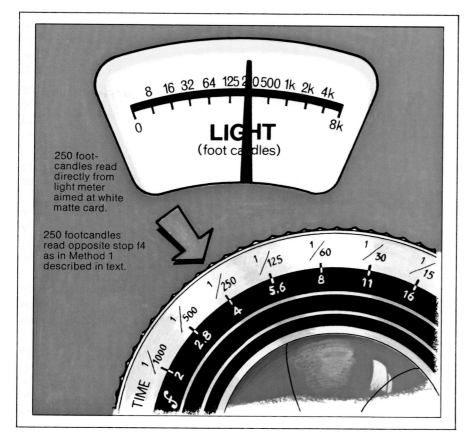

250 footcandles read directly from light meter aimed at white matte card.

250 footcandles read opposite stop f4 as in Method 1 described in text.

Photographic light meters or built-in camera meters can be used to measure footcandles by the 2 methods described below.

casts in the range of 2,000 to 3,000 lumens, which normally decreases as the tube gets older.

It is difficult to tell true light intensity visually because our eyes automatically adjust to everything they see. On a bright summer day with a slight fog that casts no discernible shadows, the meter may register more footcandles indoors than on a clear winter afternoon with a strong light-shade contrast. This is so because a gray or overcast sky reflects light, while a blue sky absorbs it. On the other hand, the back of a dark room will probably register lower on a light meter than would seem likely, because our eyes have adjusted to the relative darkness.

How to Measure Light

Some indoor gardeners are so experienced at their hobby that they have a built-in sense of available light. They instinctively know whether a certain spot has too much direct sun for a false aralia or not enough for a flowering maple. If only we all used this built-in light meter, we could dispense with the step of estimating the available light. However, since most of us haven't developed this ability, we must resort to other methods. The most accurate way of estimating light is by mechanical means, although we have provided a nonmechanical method as well.

Footcandle meter. Light meters are available that read in footcandles. The General Electric Company manufactures one (model #214), which records up to 1,000 f.c. In order to take a reading with a footcandle meter, place the meter at the same position as the surface of the leaves. Aim the plastic-covered lens toward the maximum light source. Without blocking the light or casting a shadow on the meter, check the reading on the dial. The reading will be accurate to within 10 to 15 percent, which should be adequate for your purposes.

Photographic meter. The camera's photographic meter measures the same spectrum of visible light as the footcandle meter. But the latter registers intermediate readings and is more accurate as well. However, a photographic me-

This light meter registers the number of footcandles falling on the piggyback (*Tolmeia menziesii*). It's the easiest method of measuring the actual light that reaches your plants.

ter, or a camera with a built-in light meter, will provide fairly accurate readings that can be translated into footcandles. Here are two methods:

Method 1 (illustrated on page 45): Set the film-speed dial to ASA 100 and aim the camera or hand-held meter at a sheet of matte white cardboard or paper in the proposed plant location and orient toward the maximum light source. Get close enough to the paper so that the meter or camera sees only the white paper. Be sure not to block the light or create a shadow. The shutter speed indicated opposite stop f4, reading it as a whole number, will equal the approximate number of footcandles available. For example, if the f-stop (lens opening) registers an exposure of 1/250 second, there are about 250 f.c. of light playing on the white sheet.

Method 2 (not illustrated): Set the ASA film speed at 200 and the shutter speed at 1/125 second. Focus on the white paper, as described above. Adjust the f-stop until a correct exposure is shown in the light meter. By using the table below, the f-stop will tell you how many footcandles you have:

f2.8 = 32 f.c.	f5.6 = 125 f.c.	f11 = 500 f.c.	f22 = 2,000 f.c.
f4 = 64 f.c.	f8 = 250 f.c.	f16 = 1,000 f.c.	

Light measured according to average exposure. A third method for estimating light is nonmechanical. We have done most of the work for you—just follow the diagrams for each window exposure on pages 50-56. This technique is not nearly as accurate as direct measurement, but it should be sufficient for those who are primarily interested in foliage plants and who may not have available the equipment necessary to employ the light-meter approach.

Low-intensity Light. Even the most shade tolerant of houseplants can barely exist in a dark northern corner with little light. This is probably the minimum intensity for even a maintenance level of existence. Snake plants (*Sansevieria*), *Philodendron, Dieffenbachia, Dracaena, Syngonium, Chamaedorea* and pothos will survive in extremely low light (50 to 100 f.c.). Variegated foliage frequently loses all or part of its variegation at these minimum levels.

Many rooms receive too little natural light for any plants to survive. Don't be fooled into thinking that the plants you see thriving in hotel lobbies, offices, restaurants and department stores are receiving the light they need for growth. Behind the scenes, these plants are given special treatment. A plant rental service or an employee gives the plants proper light, water, warmth and nutriment before placing them in the unfavorable environment. They appear to thrive there, but they are actually living on their reserves and will be replaced by fresh plants before they show signs of stress. Rotating plants regularly is the secret.

Generally speaking, the less light a plant gets, the lower the temperature should be. For this reason poorly lit areas should be kept as cool as possible. Plants in these locations also require less water and should be fertilized less often than their brightly lit counterparts.

The length of darkness has little effect on foliage plants—whether a plant gets 12 hours of darkness or only 6 seems to make little difference. In fact, if your heart leaved philodendron isn't getting enough light, leave the lights on longer. A shorter dark period will do it no harm and longer illumination will at least partially offset lack of intensity. A nearby lamp turned on each evening may very well be enough to maintain vigorous growth, as long as it does not produce excessive heat.

If artificial light is the *only* source of light and a foliage plant is receiving only the maintenance level of illumination in, say, a 12-hour day, then the light should be turned on for a long day every day—16 hours. If artificial light is used as a *supplement* to natural light it is best to have the lights on in the daytime to increase light intensity and to provide a more natural cycle, leaving some dark hours.

High-intensity light. Flowering plants require much higher light intensities

Washing leaves with tepid water cleans off layers of dust, actually letting more light reach the leaf surface, as well as helping to get rid of pests before they become a problem.

than foliage plants. Some will flower with a minimum of 800 f.c. over a 12-hour period, but most plants, including most annuals and perennials, require at least 1,000 f.c. for flowering to occur.

Seedlings and cuttings also need high-intensity light. They can be started in late winter under 40-watt fluorescent tubes and be ready to be set in the ground when spring arrives. Place the tubes as close as 2 inches above the sprouting seedlings and raise on chains as they grow up. Fast-growing plants such as tomatoes, zinnias, marigolds and cucumbers need a minimum of 16 hours a day of 1,000 to 1,500 f.c. for them to grow to transplanting size.

Let the Light Shine In

As the sun performs its daily ritual across the sky, the light conditions indoors constantly change: A spot that was in shadow moments before is now in full light; another area that was just in filtered sunlight is now in shadow. These fluid conditions have an enormous impact on plants. Yet most of us are only vaguely aware of the changing intensity and direction of sunlight at various times of the day. A little light awareness will help! Consider the following description of the sun's effect on the quality of light in the household.

The Three-act Play of Changing Light

The sun rises and the sun sets. In between the sun creates an ever-changing setting of light patterns and intensities. Act one of this daily performance opens with the first glow in the eastern sky. The dark room melts into shadows and these in turn give way to soft forms. The light is weak, tentative.

This glow ends suddenly when the orange glint of sunlight steals over the eastern horizon. More glimmer than real light, the sun's rays stream across the room and shimmer on the far wall. There is a pause as the sun pops above the horizon, then movement as the pattern of light moves down the wall and across the floor. Morning is here and with it the quiet radiation from our central solar body.

The eastern light is warm, yet cool—the coolest of the three exposures that receive direct sunlight. As the morning progresses the brightness of the light increases. It is the opening act of a normal day—daily, that is, except when clouds interrupt or cancel the performance.

The second act begins when the sun abandons the east and demands attention at centerstage—looking toward the south. The light is brighter now because the sun's rays have less atmosphere to penetrate before striking the earth; the direct sunlight retreats out of the room.

At midday the light is at its most intense because the sun is closest to the earth then and has the least amount of atmosphere through which to filter. The light reaches its brightest at about noon, depending on where you are located relative to the center of your time zone. Outdoors, shadows form in strong contrast to the brilliant light—this bold, dazzling, sometimes harsh noonday light. Indoors, however, at midday in the summer, the rooms of the house shielded by the roof's overhang receive no direct sunlight.

In midafternoon the final sequence in the performance opens. The sun loses its upward thrust and begins to describe its downward arc. The light, still intense, begins to move back into the room. The sun has shifted—this time from the southern side to the western exposure. The light is still bright and, as the day progresses, completely fills the room again. Spots that had been in shadow are now in direct sunlight and the heat rays shimmer on a west-facing windowsill. In the late afternoon, the color of light changes subtly from sparkling white to cream to golden yellow as the intensity drops off. Shadows lengthen and a hint of restfulness is felt.

As the sun sinks slowly below the horizon its rays reach deep into the room. Sheer curtains are a golden yellow as it crosses, ever so slowly, the western horizon. The half-light of dusk brings the room into ever-increasing darkness and our three-act play is concluded.

Notes for "Window" Graphs

The following information refers to the chart on the next 2 pages (48 and 49).

The light values shown by the *colored bars* represent the light entering a room with a single window wall, from each cardinal orientation, on the day of the summer solstice. The measurements, taken on a treeless hilltop at 37° 58' latitude, represent optimum light.

The morning and afternoon "humps" on the northern window graph are caused by low angled sunlight entering the room beneath the overhang: the *reflected* light from the side walls was sufficient to double the f.c. reading. (The meter was not in this direct light.) This effect would be less pronounced in a room with smaller windows. With less overhang a similar plateau would appear in the center portion of the southern window graph, caused by the reflected light from sun shining on the floor.

The light values shown by the *black line* are measurements made in the eastern window shown in the photographs. Light entrance into this window is delayed by a wooded hill to the East, and periodically obstructed by tree trunks and high, open foliage. Without them, the window would receive more than twice as much light. Even so, plants are exposed to about 3 times the amount of radiant energy than they would get in a good northern exposure.

It should be noted that the light intensity scale on the graph is a geometric progression, each ascending increment doubling the one below it. While the tallest bars, representing direct sunlight, are approximately double the height of the bars representing indirect or sky light, the full sunlight intensity (8,000 f.c.) is about 16 times the intensity (500 f.c.). *It is useful to realize that 4 minutes of direct sunlight provides radiant energy equal to about an hour of full sky light.* In the window photographed the direct morning sun provides about 15 times as much of the total light as the indirect sky provides.

A. 7:00 a.m. The sun is already up on the other side of the hill to the east, but not in this window.

B. 8:15 a.m. The first direct sun hits the sago palm in the window.

C. 10:15 a.m. Tree shadows cross the window: light filters through a tree canopy.

Light Values at Fixed Intervals by Exposures

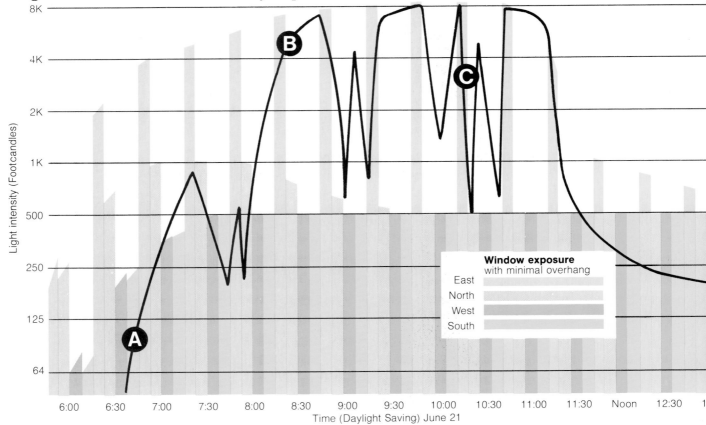

Light intensity (Footcandles)

8K
4K
2K
1K
500
250
125
64

6:00 6:30 7:00 7:30 8:00 8:30 9:00 9:30 10:00 10:30 11:00 11:30 Noon 12:30

Time (Daylight Saving) June 21

Window exposure
with minimal overhang

East
North
West
South

D. 2:30 p.m. Strong afternoon light silhouettes the plants; light on the palm comes largely from the sky all afternoon.

E. 6:00 p.m. Now the light on the hill is softer, and we can see skylight glisten on the palm fronds.

F. 7:15 p.m. A last late bit of direct light through a northwestern window passes briefly across the plants.

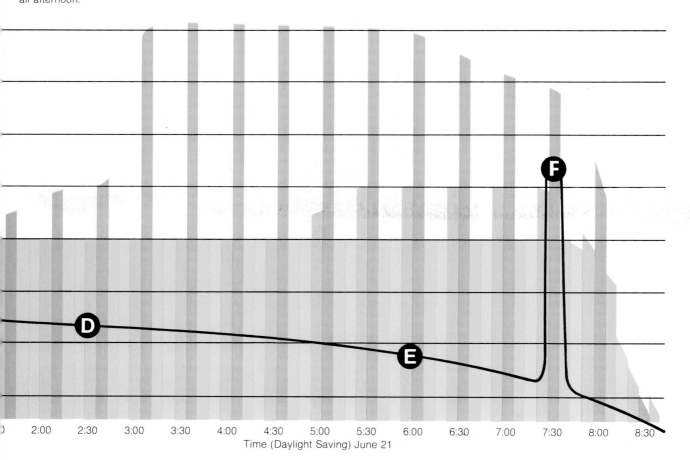

Time (Daylight Saving) June 21

2:00 2:30 3:00 3:30 4:00 4:30 5:00 5:30 6:00 6:30 7:00 7:30 8:00 8:30

Plants for a Northern Exposure

Refer to the Plant Selection Guide beginning on page 128 for specific culture and other unusual plants.

Key to code: **(B)** Bright **(H)** High humidity

Asparagus fern (*Asparagus* species)
Baby's tears (*Soleirolia soleirolii*) **(B-H)**
Caladium species
Cast iron plant (*Aspidistra elatior*)
Chinese evergreen (*Aglaonema* species)
Cobra lily (*Darlingtonia californica*)
Creeping Charlie (*Pilea nummulariifolia*) **(H)**
Creeping fig (*Ficus pumila*) **(B-H)**
Dracaena species
Dumb cane (*Dieffenbachia* species)
False aralia
   (*Dizygotheca elegantissima*) **(B-H)**
Ferns (*Adiantum, Asplenium, Cyrtomium,*
   Davallia, Nephrolepis, Phyllitis and
   Pteris species) **(H)**
Flagplant (*Acorus gramineus*) **(H)**
Goldust plant (*Aucuba japonica* 'Variegata')
Grape ivy (*Cissus rhombifolia*)
Kangaroo vine (*Cissus antarctica*)
Leopard plant (*Ligularia tussilaginea*)
Mistletoe cactus (*Rhipsalis* species) **(B-H)**
Monstera species **(H)**
Moss (*Selaginella* species) **(H)**
Mother-in-law tongue (*Sansevieria* species)
Nephthytis (*Syngonium* species)
Nerve plant (*Fittonia* species) **(H)**
Norfolk Island pine
   (*Araucaria heterophylla*) **(B)**
Orchids: *Bifrenaria* and
   Masdevallia species **(H)**
Palms (*Caryota, Chamaedorea, Howea*
   and *Rhapis* species) **(B)**
Panamiga (*Pilea involucrata*) **(H)**
Peperomia species **(B)**
Philodendron species
Pothos (*Scindapsus* and
   Epipremnum species)
Prayer plant (*Maranta* species) **(H)**
Rubber tree (*Ficus elastica*)
Sago palm (*Cycas* species)
Screw pine (*Pandanus* species) **(B)**
Spathe flower (*Spathiphyllum* species) **(H)**
Spider plant (*Chlorophytum* species)
Strawberry geranium
   (*Saxifraga stolonifera*) **(B)**
Wandering Jew (*Setcreasea, Tradescantia*
   and *Zebrina* species) **(B)**

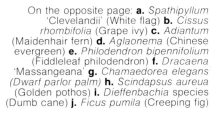

On the opposite page: **a.** *Spathipyllum* 'Clevelandii' (White flag) **b.** *Cissus rhombifolia* (Grape ivy) **c.** *Adiantum* (Maidenhair fern) **d.** *Aglaonema* (Chinese evergreen) **e.** *Philodendron bipennifolium* (Fiddleleaf philodendron) **f.** *Dracaena* 'Massangeana' **g.** *Chamaedorea elegans* (Dwarf parlor palm) **h.** *Scindapsus aureua* (Golden pothos) **i.** *Dieffenbachia* species (Dumb cane) **j.** *Ficus pumila* (Creeping fig)

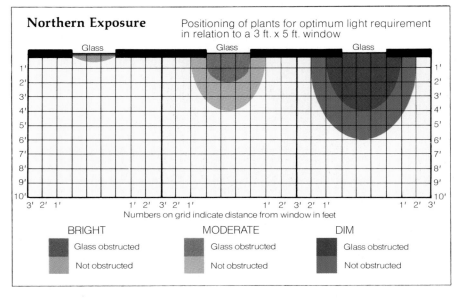

Northern Exposure   Positioning of plants for optimum light requirement in relation to a 3 ft. x 5 ft. window

Numbers on grid indicate distance from window in feet

BRIGHT
   Glass obstructed
   Not obstructed

MODERATE
   Glass obstructed
   Not obstructed

DIM
   Glass obstructed
   Not obstructed

The Cool North

Since the United States is in the northern hemisphere, it receives most of its sunlight from the south. At summer solstice (June 22), when the sun is as far north as it can go, it is just far enough north to peek into a northern window. Consequently, of the four exposures, the northern exposure receives the least light and the least heat the year around. Northern light is fairly constant throughout the day and there is less footcandle variation than there is with the other three exposures.

Because of the low light in northern windows, maintaining healthy plants there can be a challenge. A northern windowsill can register as few as 200 f.c. on a clear midwinter day. However, a wide variety of foliage plants tolerate low light and are suitable for this exposure.

The diagram above and those on the following pages are based on:
a winter noonday;
a clear atmosphere and a strong sun; and
a 38 to 42° belt of latitude across the United States, which includes Washington, Philadelphia, New York, Boston, Detroit, Chicago, St. Louis, Denver, Salt Lake City and San Francisco.

The values shown are higher in other seasons and for those areas south of latitude 38°. They would be lower at any other time of day or north of latitude 42°.

The dim-moderate-bright values are based on these f.c. ranges:
dim light = 50 to 200 f.c.;
moderate light = 200 to 500 f.c.;
bright light = 500 to 1,000 f.c.

They are the same categories used to describe the minimum lighting requirements for plants in the charts on pages 128-138.

In general, plants grown particularly for their green foliage will tolerate a northern exposure, even if they prefer brighter light. Plants with colored foliage often prefer somewhat brighter light, and lose some of their color when placed in a northern location. And plants grown for their flowers usually need a brighter exposure than a northern one. Like all generalizations, however, you will find exceptions. If plants grow leggy while being grown on a northern windowsill, move them to an eastern one, or supplement the natural light with a fluorescent kind.

Remember that many plants will survive where they will not grow. You may want to use your northern exposure for a plant display area but actually grow your plants in an area with higher light levels. One day or a week in the northern exposure will not change any plant or cause unsightly growth.

Plants for an Eastern Exposure

Key to code: **(B)** Bright   **(F)** Filtered sun
(H) High humidity   **(C)** Cool

African violets (*Saintpaulia* species)
Aluminum plant (*Pilea cadierei*) **(H)**
Anthurium species
Aralia, Japanese (*Fatsia japonica*) **(C)**
Artillery plant (*Pilea microphylla*) **(H)**
Asparagus fern (*Asparagus* species)
Avocado (*Persea americana*) **(B-H)**
Azalea (*Rhododendron* species) **(B-H)**
Baby's tears (*Soleirolia soleirolii*) **(H)**
Begonia species **(B-H-C)**
Bromeliads (many species) **(H)**
Calla lily (*Zantedeschia* species) **(B)**
Cast iron plant (*Aspidistra elatior*)
Chenille plant (*Acalypha hispida*)
Chinese evergreen (*Aglaonema* species)
Chinese lemon (*Citrus limon* 'Meyer') **(B)**
Christmas cactus
   (*Schlumbergera* species) **(B-H)**
Clerodendrum species
Coleus species
Columnea species
Creeping Charlie (*Pilea nummulariifolia*) **(H)**
Cyperus species **(C)**
Devil's backbone (*Pedilanthus tithymaloides*)
Dieffenbachia species
Dracaena species
False aralia (*Dizygotheca elegantissima*) **(H)**
Ferns (many species) **(H-F-C)**
Ficus species
Flame violet (*Episcia* species) **(H)**
Flowering maple (*Abutilon* species) **(B)**
Fuchsia species **(B-H-C)**
Geranium (*Pelargonium* species) **(B)**
Ginger (many species) **(B-H)**
Gloxinia (*Sinningia* species)
Goldfish (*Nematanthus* species) **(H)**
Grape ivy (*Cissus rhombifolia*)
Hawaiian ti (*Cordyline terminalis*)
Hibiscus rosa-sinensis **(B-H)**
Ivy (*Hedera* species) **(C)**
Kangaroo vine (*Cissus antarctica*)
Lipstick vine (*Aeschynanthus* species)
Ming aralia (*Polyscias* species) **(B-H)**
Mistletoe cactus (*Rhipsalis* species) **(H)**
Moses-in-the-cradle
   (*Rhoeo spathacea*) **(C)**
Moss (*Selaginella* species) **(H-F)**
Mother-in-law tongue (*Sansevieria*)
Myrtle (*Myrtus communis*) **(B)**
Nephthytis (*Syngonium* species)
Nerve plant (*Fittonia* species) **(H)**
Norfolk Island pine (*Araucaria heterophylla*)
Orchid cactus (*Epiphyllum* species)
Orchids (many species) **(B-H)**
Palms (many species) **(B-C)**
Papyrus (*Cyperus papyrus*) **(C-M)**
Peperomia species **(H)**
Philodendron species
Piggyback (*Tolmiea menziesii*)
Pink polkadot
   (*Hypoestes phyllostachya*)

Pocketbook (*Calceolaria* species) **(C)**
Ponytail (*Beaucarnea recurvata*) **(B)**
Pothos (*Scindapsus* and
   Epipremnum species)
Prayer plant (*Maranta* species) **(H)**
Schefflera (*Brassaia* and
   Schefflera species)
Spathe flower (*Spathiphyllum* species)
Spider plant (*Chlorophytum* species) **(H-C)**
String-of-pearls (*Senecio rowleyanus*)
Succulents (many species)
Swedish ivy (*Plectranthus* species) **(H-C)**
Tree ivy (*Fatshedera lizei*) **(H)**
Velvet plant (*Gynura aurantiaca*) **(B-H)**
Wandering Jew (*Setcreasea, Tradescantia*
   and *Zebrina* species) **(B-H-C)**
Wax plant (*Hoya* species) **(B-H)**
Zebra plant (*Aphelandra* species)

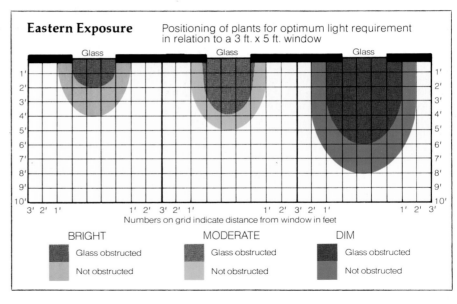

Eastern Exposure   Positioning of plants for optimum light requirement in relation to a 3 ft. x 5 ft. window

Numbers on grid indicate distance from window in feet

BRIGHT   MODERATE   DIM

Glass obstructed   Glass obstructed   Glass obstructed
Not obstructed   Not obstructed   Not obstructed

The Obliging East

The eastern exposure receives direct morning light from sunrise until nearly midday. Footcandle readings can reach from 5,000 to 8,000. As the morning progresses, the direct sun recedes from the room. Eaves or overhanging foliage outside may hasten this process. An eastern room is cooler than ones situated to the south or west because the house absorbs less radiant heat. Most plants will tolerate some direct sun from an eastern direction, particularly early in the morning.

Most plants grown indoors prefer an eastern exposure. Light from the east is cooler than that from the south or west, and is, therefore, less dehydrating. The early rays of the sun act as an alarm clock, awakening the plants to their day's task: photosynthesis. Many gardeners first try an eastern setting for any plant about which light preference is in question. This list, necessarily, includes only the most available plants for indoor gardeners, but could be expanded tenfold if space permitted.

On the opposite page:
a. *Dizygotheca elegantissima* (False aralia)
b. *Nephrolepis exaltata* 'Bostoniensis'
(Boston fern) **c.** *Ficus benjamina* (Weeping fig) **d.** *Dracaena reflexa* **e.** *Begonia rex* (Rex begonia) **f.** *Dryopteris* (Wood fern) **g.** *Cordyline terminalis* (Hawaiian ti) **h.** *Tolmiea menziesii* (Piggyback) **i.** *Saintpaulia ionantha* (African violet) **j.** *Polyscias* (Ming aralia) **k.** *Aeschynanthus radicans* (Lipstick vine) **l.** *Sinningia speciosa* (Gloxinia) **m.** *Tradescantia* Wandering Jew)

Plants for a Southern Exposure

Key to code: (**H**) High humidity
(**C**) Cool   (**F**) Filtered sun

Amaryllis (*Hippeastrum* species)
Annuals and vegetables (many species)
Aralia, Japanese (*Fatsia japonica*)
Asparagus fern (*Asparagus* species)
Avocado (*Persea americana*) (**H**)
Azalea (*Rhododendron* species) (**H-C**)
Bamboo (*Bambusa* species) (**H**)
Banana (*Musa* species)
Begonia (fibrous rooted and wax,
    B. semperflorens) (**H-F**)
Bleeding heart (*Clerodendrum* species)
Bromeliads (many species)
Cacti (many species) (**H**)
Calla lily (*Zantedeschia* species)
Camellia species
Chenille plant (*Acalypha hispida*)
Citrus species
Coffee (*Coffea* species) (**H**)
Coleus species
Double-decker plant (*Sinningia verticillata*)
Elephant ears (*Colocasia* species)
Ferns (*Alsophila, Cyathea* and
    Polypodium species) (**H**)
Flame violet (*Episcia* species) (**H**)
Flame-of-the-woods (*Ixora* species)
Flowering tobacco (*Nicotiana alata*
    'Grandiflora')
Gardenia jasminoides (**H**)
Geranium (*Pelargonium* species)
Heavenly bamboo (*Nandina domestica*)
Hibiscus rosa-sinensis
Ivy (*Hedera* species)
Kaffir lily (*Clivia* species)
Lily-of-the-Nile (*Agapanthus* species)
Lipstick vine (*Aeschynanthus* species)
Myrtle (*Myrtus communis*)
Natal plum (*Carissa grandiflora*)
Pink polkadot (*Hypoestes phyllostachya*) (**H**)
Olive (*Olea europaea*)
Orchids (*Aerides* and *Dendrobium* species)
Oxalis species (**H**)
Palms (*Caryota, Chamaerops, Howea* and
    Veitchia species)
Papyrus (*Cyperus papyrus*) (**H-F**)
Parlor ivy (*Senecio mikanioides*) (**C**)
Passion flower (*Passiflora* species) (**H**)
Pepper (*Capsicum* species)
Pittosporum tobira
Podocarpus species
Ponytail (*Beaucarnea recurvata*)
Privet (*Ligustrum japonicum*)
Rainbow flower (*Achimenes* species)
Schefflera (*Brassaia* and
    Schefflera species) (**H**)
Shrimp plant (*Justicia brandegeana*) (**H**)
Singapore holly (*Malpighia coccigera*)
Spider plant (*Chlorophytum* species) (**F**)
String-of-pearls (*Senecio rowleyanus*) (**H**)
Succulents (many species)
Swedish ivy (*Plectranthus* species) (**H**)
Sweet olive (*Osmanthus fragrans*) (**H-C**)
Treevine (*Cissus discolor*)
Winter creeper (*Euonymous radicans*)
Zephyr lily (*Zephyranthes* species)

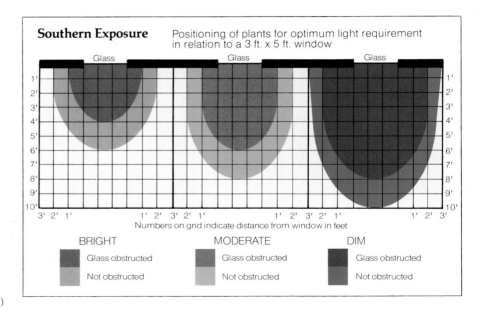

The Sunny South

The seasonal variation in southern light is greater than in any other exposure. Fortunately for the indoor gardener, the low winter sun streams across the room for most of the daylight hours. On a bright, sunny winter day the southern room becomes your greenhouse. In the summer, when the sun is farther north than in the winter, the sun rises at a sharp angle in the morning and is high in the sky by noon. Consequently, direct sunlight streams into a southern window only at midday. If there is a wide overhang outside, the sun may not enter the room at all.

The amount of light that enters a southern window will be only a portion of the available light outdoors on a clear day. The sun at noon on a summer day may register as many as 10,000 f.c.—more if light reflects off of buildings as well. Indoors, however, on the same sunny day, a southern window with wide eaves outside will receive about the same amount of light as a window with a northern exposure.

Southern and western exposures are interchangeable for most plants. In the winter, direct light may need to be diffused and more humidity, perhaps some cooling, may be required. With these precautions, many plants, certainly more than this list indicates, may be placed in a south-facing area. In fact, with care, all but those with a definite northern preference may be grown in a southern room in the winter. In the summer, most plants that are happy with an eastern exposure will do well with a southern exposure. Those plants listed for a western exposure that require filtered western light will also thrive in the south in summertime.

On the opposite page:
a. *Beaucarnea recurvata* (Ponytail)
b. *Citrofortunella mitis* (Calamondin orange)
c. *Echeveria* **d.** *Nandina domestica*
(Heavenly bamboo) **e.** *Echeveria affinis*
f. *and* **g.** *Coleus blumei* **h.** *Rhododendron*
species (Azalea) **i.** *Coffea arabica* (Coffee)
j. *Sedum morganianum* (Donkey's tail)
k. *Kalanchoe blossfeldiana* **l.** *Echinocactus grusonii*
(Golden barrel cactus)

Plants for a Western Exposure

Key to code: **(B)** Bright **(H)** High humidity
(C) Cool **(F)** Filtered sun

African violets (*Saintpaulia* species) **(H-F-C)**
Algerian ivy (*Hedera canariensis*) **(F-C)**
Aluminum plant (*Pilea cadierei*) **(H)**
Amaryllis (*Hippeastrum* species)
Annuals and vegetables (many species) **(B)**
Aralia (*Fatsia japonica*)
Artillery plant (*Pilea microphylla*) **(H)**
Asparagus fern (*Asparagus* species)
Avocado (*Persea americana*) **(H)**
Bamboo (*Bambusa* species) **(H)**
Banana (*Musa* species)
Begonia species
Bleeding heart (*Clerodendrum* species)
Bromeliads (many species) **(H-C)**
Cacti (many species)
Camellia species
Cast iron plant (*Aspidistra elatior*)
Chenille plant (*Acalypha hispida*)
Citrus species **(C)**
Coffee (*Coffea* species)
Coleus species **(F)**
Columnea species **(H-F-C)**
Creeping Charlie
   (*Pilea nummulariifolia*) **(H-F-C)**
Croton (*Codiaeum* species)
Elephant ears (*Colocasia* species)
Ferns (*Alsophila, Cyathea* and
   Platycerium species) **(H-F-C)**
Ficus species **(H-F)**
Firecracker flower (*Crossandra* species)
Flame violet (*Episcia* species) **(H)**
Flame-of-the-woods (*Ixora* species)
Flowering tobacco (*Nicotiana alata*)
Geranium (*Pelargonium* species)
Goldfish (*Nematanthus* species) **(H)**
Lily-of-the-Nile (*Agapanthus* species)
Ming aralia (*Polyscias* species) **(H-F)**
Mother-in-law's tongue
   (*Sansevieria* species) **(F)**
Myrtle (*Myrtus communis*)
Nerve plant (*Fittonia* species) **(H)**
Orchids (*Dendrobium* species) **(H)**
Oxalis species **(H-C)**
Palms (*Chamaerops, Howea, Livistona* and
   Rhapis species) **(H-F-C)**
Parlor ivy (*Senecio mikanioides*) **(C)**
Peperomia species **(H-F)**
Piggyback *(Tolmiea menziesii)*
Pittosporum species
Rainbow flower (*Achimenes* species)
Rosary vine (*Ceropegia woodii*)
Sago palm (*Cycas* species) **(H)**
Schefflera (*Brassaia* and *Schefflera* species)
Spider plant (*Chlorophytum* species) **(H-F-C)**
Succulents (many species)
Swedish ivy (*Plectranthus* species) **(H-F-C)**
Tree ivy (*Fatshedera lizei*) **(H-C)**
Velvet plant (*Gynura aurantiaca*) **(H-F)**
Wax plant (*Hoya* species)
Zebra plant (*Aphelandra* species)

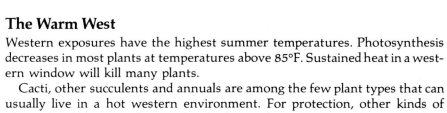

Western Exposure — Positioning of plants for optimum light requirement in relation to a 3 ft. x 5 ft. window

Numbers on grid indicate distance from window in feet

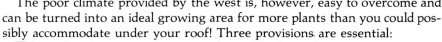
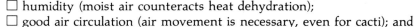

BRIGHT — Glass obstructed / Not obstructed
MODERATE — Glass obstructed / Not obstructed
DIM — Glass obstructed / Not obstructed

The Warm West

Western exposures have the highest summer temperatures. Photosynthesis decreases in most plants at temperatures above 85°F. Sustained heat in a western window will kill many plants.

Cacti, other succulents and annuals are among the few plant types that can usually live in a hot western environment. For protection, other kinds of plants should be moved 2 or 3 feet back into the room where less intense late afternoon rays can do little harm. This exposure receives about the same duration of light as the eastern exposure does-about 4 hours of direct sun a day.

The poor climate provided by the west is, however, easy to overcome and can be turned into an ideal growing area for more plants than you could possibly accommodate under your roof! Three provisions are essential:
☐ humidity (moist air counteracts heat dehydration);
☐ good air circulation (air movement is necessary, even for cacti); and
☐ curtaining (it filters out the scorching rays). From November to March, it is not necessary to curtain a western exposure for plants that require bright light.

Not only does light vary by exposure and season, it also varies by elevation and latitude. Light intensity is much higher in the mountains than at sea level because the atmosphere is thinner there and less light is filtered out before striking the earth. Indirect light through a window may be less intense at these elevations, since the deeper blue of the sky reflects less light.

Note that while air conditioning provides some movement of cool air, it is also very drying. So when an air conditioner is running, pay special attention to adding humidity.

a. *Cissus antarctica* (Kangaroo vine)
b. *Araucaria heterophylla* (Norfolk Island pine) **c.** *Pilea microphylla* (Artillery fern) **d.** *Lilium* hybrid **e.** *Schefflera octophylla* **f.** *Codiaeum* species (Croton) **g.** *Sansevieria trifasciata* (Mother-in-law's tongue) **h.** *Ficus elastica* (Rubber plant) **i.** *Aechmea fasciata* (Living vase) **j.** *Fittonia verschaffeltii argyroneura* (Nerve plant)

Modifying Natural Light

The amount or distribution of light entering a room through windows may not meet the requirements of particular houseplants. However, a number of techniques and devices can be employed in the average household that will improve your plants' environment. Although some of the ideas presented here are self-evident—they should be taken as reminders—they may literally make the difference between night and day for a roomful of plants.

Open the curtains, shades and shutters. One obvious piece of advice is to open the curtains or shutters and raise the shades each morning on arising. Or even better, open the curtains in living room, dining room and kitchen before you go to bed so that plants may take advantage of the sun's first morning rays. Heavy curtains can bar all effective light as far as plant growth is concerned, as do pulled shades. With shutters or Venetian blinds a common mistake is to adjust the movable louvers to one position, forgetting that the sun's angle changes throughout the day. It is better to open the blinds completely.

Prune outdoor plants. Large shrubs or trees may block sunlight all or part of the day. Mature trees can steal all of the light away if you let them. Thinning and pruning can admit the light that your prize Indian laurel fig needs and will improve the outdoor tree's health, too. Sometimes the problem may be solved by tying branches back so that needed light can pass through. This can often be done in such a way, with the use of dark colored wire, that your rearrangement is not evident. You may want to consider removing a tree that has passed its prime and is in decline and replacing it with a smaller specimen.

Keep windows and plants clean. It is surprising how much light can be blocked from plants when the glass is dirty. Regular window washing is important to plants' health. But it does not do much good to have sparkling clean windows if the foliage is dusty. Washing or wiping dust from leaves can increase a plant's exposure to light considerably. (See page 46.)

Consider awnings and overhangs. When constructing or remodeling your home, remember that exterior architectural features can block the amount of light that gets inside. Select awnings that can be raised or lowered easily and can help modify the light falling on plants indoors.

Left: Sheer curtains serve two purposes: They filter out harsh afternoon sun and reflect a more even light throughout the room.

Right: Shutters can adjust the amount and directness of the light that comes through windows. For maximum light, remember to open the shutters every day.

Modifying Interior Light

The amount of light within a room can also be modified. This entails redistributing the light that enters at the windows and may be crucial in a room with only a small opening. A large window naturally admits more light than a small window; there is more direct sunlight and therefore more internally reflected light within the room. The intensity of sunlight on a windowsill plant is the same, regardless of the size of the window. But the intensity begins to differ as one moves away from the glass. The brightness of the light decreases much more rapidly in a room with a small window than in one with a large window. A 2,000 f.c. reading obtained on the wall next to a glass window may decrease to 1,000 f.c. only 10 feet into the room. That same 2,000 f.c. might decrease to as little as 200 f.c. when measured 10 feet away from a common, small double-hung window—down to only 20 percent as much! There are several tactics the homeowner may employ to guard against footcandle loss.

Sheer curtains can act as thousands of tiny reflectors, dispersing moderately strong light into areas farther away from the window than it would reach otherwise. While they will decrease the intensity of light in the sunlit area, they will increase the amount of light farther back into the room because of their reflective quality. A white nylon net curtain might be expected to decrease direct sunlight from 8,000 to 2,000 f.c. in the area immediately behind the window, but increase the readings from 125 f.c. to 250 f.c. 5 feet away.

Wall coverings. A fairly new product on the market is aluminized Mylar, a thin plastic sheet to which a thin coat of aluminum has been applied by a vacuum process. This material is highly reflective and provides a good method of distributing light into the darker parts of rooms. A related product is metalized wallpaper, which does not reflect as much light as aluminized Mylar, but may be more compatible with the interior design.

Light hued paint reflects more than darker tones. White is the most effective, of course, and can add as much as 150 f.c. into a dark room with the same light source. Matte white paint will reflect ¾ or more of the light that strikes it —see the accompanying table showing the reflective quality of commonly used materials.

This homemade folding screen, with the frame painted matte white and with inset Mylar panels, did a good job of reflecting light from the window across the room onto plants on the table. A floor-standing screen is an alternative for large plants.

Mirrors and mirror reflectors. Mirrors and mirrorized walls can direct and distribute light into an otherwise dark room. Mirrored tiles are readily available. In addition to making light more even in a room, they will visually expand the size of your interior garden.

However, using mirrored surfaces to reflect direct light from the sun into a room can present many difficulties. The amount of light that can be reflected from a flat mirrored surface can be no larger than the size of the mirror itself. Mirrors have to be directed in exactly the right way, and the right way changes rapidly as the earth revolves into and away from the sunlight. Then there is the further problem of how to reflect the sun into the room without having the full glare in your eyes somewhere inside the room.

Considering these problems, it was a surprise to find one example of the use of full sun with mirror reflectors to enhance inside light. This reflector arrangement is installed on a window that faces almost due south. In the summer the roof overhang blocks direct sunlight from the window. A hinged outside mirror, 6 feet long and 14 inches wide along the bottom of the window, reflects light upward through the window; the angle is adjusted so that this light is confined to an area directly above the window. Only by bringing your face very close to the window can you see a direct reflection of the sun. Inside the room above the window, a mirror of equal size reflects the light directly down onto the plant growing area.

With these two mirrors the plant area receives over 2 hours of midday sun. The addition of two vertical mirrors on each side of the window to pick up and reflect earlier and later sunlight extends this to about 4 hours, enough to grow most outdoor garden plants.

It would be advantageous to make the inside mirrors a few inches wider than the outside mirrors so that the shallow arc pattern of the sun's reflected movement could be fully used. With three mirrors the light pattern would make three overlapping transits of the planting area. The outside mirror and

The illustrations and photographs on these two pages show how a combination of mirrors—inside and out—reflect light on indoor plants.

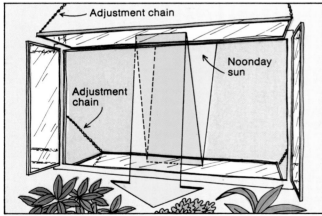

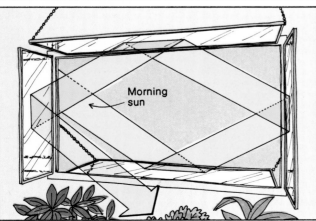

the top inside mirror must be hinged so that the angle can be easily adjusted. Such an adjustment to changing sun angle should be made each week.

The outside mirror is supported by link chains with long turnbuckles at the upper wall attachment points and strong springs at the lower wall attachment points, allowing for angle adjustment. A double turnbuckle arrangement on each chain, without the springs, would provide more positive resistance to movement in strong winds.

Without the inside mirrors, just the bright patch of sunlight directed onto the white ceiling is enough to double the light intensity in the center of the room 8 feet from the window. In the winter, when direct sunlight comes through the windows, the combined direct or reflected light is the equivalent of desert light, even with the loss from the window glass and the mirrors.

First you have to have a window facing due south. Adding an hour of direct reflected sunlight will double the radiant energy on plants receiving only reflected light from the sky. Perhaps there are other window orientations where modifications of this kind would work. Attach a shaving mirror to a board and run it out the window—adjust it to put the bright circle of reflection on the ceiling and see where it moves for an hour or two. The least you may come up with is an unusual seasonal sundial on the ceiling.

Evaluating Available Light

Now that you have a general understanding of the principles of light and exposure and a feel for the way plants react to light, what is the next step? It is to perform an environmental inventory of your living space. This will consist of a series of checklists for each lighting situation. Refer to the charts on pages 128-138. Apply them to your existing houseplants first to make certain that each has an optimum lighting situation. Add supplemental artificial illumination where necessary. If possible, provide extra lighting in places in your home that have differing temperature ranges, so that you will have environments for the broadest possible variety of plant types. With checklists in hand as you add or replace plants, you will be able to make sensible selections based on your actual light and heat conditions. You will finally be able to cast more light on indoor plants.

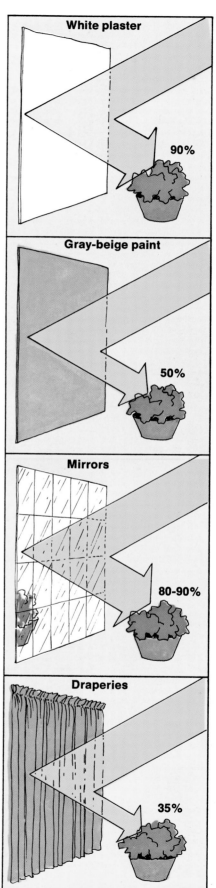

White plaster

90%

Gray-beige paint

50%

Mirrors

80-90%

Draperies

35%

USING ARTIFICIAL LIGHT

If you don't have enough natural light, supplement or substitute it with artificial light for healthier plants.

Assume you have made an effort to increase your natural light by one or more of the means discussed in the preceding chapter. You may have:

- ☐ painted your rooms matte (flat) white;
- ☐ invested in curtains and shades that open all the way;
- ☐ trimmed or removed exterior foliage that was blocking light;
- ☐ repositioned your plants so they receive the maximum amount of light.

And still that schefflera next to the sofa isn't growing and appears weak and spindly. You've fed and watered it properly, but it just isn't doing well. Not enough light. *It's too dark* in the room.

Or you are a gesneriad fancier. Your friends have been growing prize African violets for years, while yours have produced few blooms. But the adjacent building blocks out most of the sun's radiant energy. *Not enough light.*

Or you want to get a jump on spring by starting seedlings indoors. But because you live in Minnesota you are not as fortunate as those in Texas, who enjoy longer and sunnier winter days and can make good use of a kitchen window garden. Your kitchen just *doesn't get enough light.*

Or you have always enjoyed that spectacular view from your apartment—it's the toast of your friends. But having a northern exposure has limited the plants you can grow. There just isn't enough light to bring your cattleya orchid into flower or to support a healthy weeping fig. *It's too dark.*

Turn Dark into Light

Artificial lighting can solve these problems and many others. Plants can grow and bloom in a situation where artificial light is their sole energy source. Or, more naturally, artificial light can be used to supplement sunlight. When the day shortens in autumn, most plants will have a slower growth rate. However, artificial light can be employed to extend the growing season.

Any type of artificial light will help a plant, even if it is your floor lamp turned on for only a few hours each evening. Bright overhead lights will go a long way in making up light deficiency for tall plants. But in a room that is poorly lighted by the sun, ordinary house lighting will not be enough. Specialized lighting will have to be installed. It can make a garden of the dimmest room where no foliage plants would ordinarily survive and can allow flowering plants to blossom in places that would normally support only foliage plants.

Some commercial growers have used artificial lighting for years to help produce a quality and quantity of flowers that they would be unable to achieve in any other fashion. Others use carefully timed periods of artificial light to either stimulate or retard flowering. Chrysanthemums and flowering kalanchoe are prime examples of widely grown commercial flowering plants that are completely controllable as to flowering time by the application of controlled lighting. Everyone knows of the short day requirements to bring poinsettias into bloom for the Christmas holidays. The bedding plant industry

An inverted clay pot inside a macramé hanger is used as a lamp shade for an incandescent bulb that also lights a spider plant. Several hanging plants with lights may provide all the evening illumination needed in a room.

Clamp-on incandescent sockets with reflectors provide a temporary plant-growth light. Low-light plants can thrive under such light.

uses artificial lighting to start seedlings. And for over a decade indoor gardening enthusiasts have established often elaborate setups in basements, attics and livingroom bookshelves.

Artificial light does not exactly duplicate sunlight; its colors are present in different proportions. But certain types of artificial light can faithfully induce the same natural responses in plants. Not all plants will thrive under artificial light, since this light is not nearly as intense as natural sunlight. However, a vast number of plants require only a moderate amount of sunlight in nature and will perform quite well indoors under lights. As long as the required light waves are present in the proper proportions, the *source* of the light is unimportant.

Since fluorescent lights are rich in foliage-producing blue rays, plants grown primarily for their foliage effect can subsist happily on fluorescents alone. Plants that flower, however, require red and far-red energy as well—needing supplemental sunlight, incandescent light or full-spectrum fluorescent light if they are to bloom well.

Artificial light can be produced by a broad array of lamps. We are concerned here only with those fixtures and lamps that are adaptable to indoor gardening use.

Incandescent Light

The most common incandescent bulbs are the bulbs used every day in the home. This bulb consists of a tungsten filament wire that has high resistance to electricity. Electrical current flowing through this high resistance causes the filament to heat up and glow, thus producing visible light.

Incandescent light is rich in red and far-red light, which is indispensable for flowering and other plant processes. In fact, incandescent light possesses the same proportion of red and far-red rays as sunlight, although it is vastly less intense. However, it does not contain enough of the blue and violet rays of the spectrum; therefore, incandescent light is not suitable as a sole energy source for complete plant growth. It can be used to supplement daylight when the light deficiency is minimal. A Boston fern or a *Spathiphyllum* on a side table can get needed supplementary light from an ordinary 75-watt lamp burning 3 or 4 hours a night.

Incandescent light has distinct advantages for lighting individual plants. Single bulb fixtures are readily available and through the use of reflector floodlights or spotlights concentrated beams of light can easily be aimed exactly where the light is wanted. Reflector bulbs are available in 75, 150, and 300 watt sizes so there is no trouble in adjusting light intensity for a single light fixture.

Incandescents also give off a considerable amount of heat. This heat can be damaging to plants if the light source is too close. A rule of thumb is: *If your hand feels warm when held at the foliage closest to the light source, the plant is too close. Generally speaking, it is best to keep the tops of plants at least a foot away from incandescent sources.* Naturally, the lamp should not be placed too far away from the plant, either. The light reaching the plant will decrease with the square of the distance that it is removed. That is, a plant 2 feet away from a light source will receive only ¼ as much light as it would if it were 1 foot away.

An easy way to reduce heat is to use several smaller bulbs instead of one large one. This distributes the heat over a larger area, allows the lamps to be placed closer to the plants and provides more even distribution of light. If this is impractical, a shield of glass or transparent plastic will absorb or reflect a large amount of heat while allowing nearly all of the light to pass through to the plant. The shield should be placed several inches away from the lamp.

Another method of avoiding heat problems is to use reflectorized incandescent lamps such as Cool Beam or Cool Lux. These bulbs contain a silverized reflecting surface that reflects light downward but conducts heat upward. The heat projected downward by this method may be reduced by 50 percent or more. A word of warning: These bulbs should always be used in a ceramic socket, since a regular socket will soon burn out.

Fluorescent Light

Fluorescent lamps are familiar to us as the ones commonly used in offices, factories and public places. Introduced in 1938, these lamps have become very popular because they are economical, long-lasting, and distribute light evenly. They are more energy efficient than incandescent lamps. A fluorescent lamp of the same wattage as an incandescent lamp emits 2½ to 3 times as much light. The lifetime of a fluorescent tube is about 15 to 20 times that of an incandescent bulb. Thus, in the long run, fluorescent lighting is much more economical than incandescent.

The long tubular glass bulb of fluorescent lamps is coated on the inside with a phosphor. The type of phosphor determines the "color" of the light given off. The mixture of phosphorescent chemicals determines the "mix" of the various color wavelengths. *The visible color, however, is not indicative of the proportion of blue and red waves given off.* The bulb contains a blend of inert gases, including argon, neon or krypton, and a minute quantity of mercury vapor, sealed in a low-pressure vacuum. There are two electrodes, one at each end of the tube. Electrical power induces a current to flow between the electrodes in the form

This varied begonia collection thrives with fluorescents as the only source of light.

of an electrical arc, which stimulates the phosphor and emits energy in the form of light. *This emission is stronger in the center of the tube than at the ends.*

The electricity is regulated by a ballast, which is a small transformer that reduces the current in the tube to the operating level required by that particular lamp. The ballast is usually contained in the fixture and emits most of the small amount of heat given off by a fluorescent lamp. In most fixtures it is positioned far enough away from the bulb so that plants can actually touch a fluorescent bulb without having adverse effects.

In most home-lighting circumstances, the heat given off by the ballast is not a problem unless a great number of large fixtures are used in one small area so that the overall room temperature is raised. If an individual fixture seems to be radiating too much heat downward, the ballast can be removed from the metal tray that houses it and a piece of asbestos can be placed between ballast and tray. When a number of lamps must be located together, making heat buildup a problem, the ballasts can be installed away from the lamps themselves. This should really be done by an experienced electrician.

A ballast uses about 10 watts of electricity for every 40 watts used by the lamp itself. This is important to figure in when large installations are being contemplated, so that the circuits do not become overloaded. Ballasts normally last from 10 to 12 years. When they burn out they sometimes smoke and give off a noxious chemical odor. They can be easily replaced without professional help by the average homeowner; check with your local electrical or hardware dealer.

A fluorescent tube is held in the fixture by pins at both ends of the tube. There are four types of pins:

☐ the 2-pin (medium bi-pin) is the most common, usually found on bulbs with low wattages, up to 90 watts;

☐ the 1-pin, used on bulbs with a narrow diameter and for intermediate wattages;

☐ the recessed double contact pin, used on bulbs with high wattages; and

☐ the 4-pin, used on circular bulbs with various wattages.

Fluorescent lamps don't "turn on" the way incandescent lamps do. The bulb's cathodes must be warm before an arc can be struck through the lamp. The starting process is a major factor in bulb wear. A pair of 40-watt, cool-white fluorescent bulbs will last about twice as long if burned continuously than if burned 3 hours a day because of the energy and wear used in the starting process.

Fluorescent lamps are available in various colors:

White	*Sign white*	*Deluxe cool white*
Cool white	*Living white*	*Supermarket white*
Warm white	*Soft white*	*Merchandising white*
Daylight	*Deluxe warm white*	

"Color" refers to the *quality* of the light given off, rather than to the bulb's temperature. The cool-white tube is the traditional lamp used by indoor gardeners. Because most fluorescent light is not as attractive to the eye as incandescent light, many people leave fluorescents on during the daytime so that natural daylight can help to offset the harshness of the light or because no one is at home to observe it. This practice adds only a few cents a day to the electrical bill. The deluxe warm white is the most flattering fluorescent to complexions and home furnishings.

A bewildering array of fluorescent lamps is available. Sylvania, General Electric and Westinghouse are the largest manufacturers. Their catalogs list a full range of sizes, shapes, colors and wattages. The chart on page 69 goes into some detail, indicating representative bulbs from major manufacturers for the benefit of the indoor gardener.

Although initially more expensive than incandescent bulbs, fluourescent lamps form the backbone of gardening by artificial light. As we have discussed,

Fluorescent tubes hidden underneath the window valance supplement sunlight in this indoor hanging tomato garden.

they throw off so little heat they can be placed very close to the plants. They can be positioned as close as 1 inch from many blooming plants, although 6 to 9 inches is more advisable. Nevertheless, lamps should not be placed more than 18 inches away from the top of a plant with any expectation of flowering, unless the lamps have a high output. For best flowering, fluorescent lights should operate 10 to 18 hours a day if they are the sole light source.

Timers are a great help in keeping lighting on schedule, particularly when you are away from home. Timers should be fully adjustable to any period in a full 24 hours and should be able to carry the wattage demanded. Low-cost timers are available in most hardware stores. Many people burn their lights regularly on timers when they are away to discourage burglars, so the light may as well benefit the plants at the same time.

Because fluorescents, like incandescents, "blacken" with age and lose light efficiency, some experts recommend that bulbs be replaced when they reach 70 percent of their stated life, usually listed on the bulb package or label. At this point they provide about 15 percent less light than when new. Noting the installation date by grease pencil on the end of the tube will assist in its timely replacement. A "flickering" lamp is about to burn out and should be replaced. Indoor gardeners who have banks of lamps often stagger the lamp replacement to prevent "light shock" to plants accustomed to dimming light.

There are three common methods of increasing the amount of fluorescent light: add more fixtures, reflect more light onto the plants or move the plants closer to the lamps. Using longer tubes will increase light *because there is considerable light loss at the ends of tubes.* There is twice as much light 1 foot away from a fluorescent light source as there is 2 feet away. Fluorescent tubes can be dimmed by rheostats only if special dimming ballasts are installed. These are available for use with 30 and 40-watt tubes.

Ordinary fluorescent light in the right intensities can promote lush foliage growth, even if not a drop of sunlight is available. But, like incandescent light, it is short on certain parts of the spectrum needed for an entirely balanced plant life. All common fluorescent output is very high in blue light, which promotes foliage growth, and is extremely low in red and far-red light, which promotes flowering.

The fireplace can be a summer garden. Here plant-growth fluorescents are installed inside the chimney. Mylar covered panels cover the sides and back for extra reflectance. A glass or plastic screen can be added over the opening for a terrariumlike atmosphere.

Attach spring-loaded pole to back of cross piece. It will hold your plant-light upright between floor and ceiling.

5"

2"

7' 6"

Fluorescent fixture with two 40 watt lamps 72" long

1" x 8" redwood boards on each side—stained on the outside, painted white on the inside, and painted black on the edges.

A vertical plant-growth fixture for tall plants can be easily constructed. Finish the sides to fit your interior design scheme.

Light in Proper Proportion

There are two ways of providing light in the proper proportions to support all plant processes while still bypassing the sun:

☐ Combine fluorescent and incandescent light.
☐ Use "plant growth" lamps.

Combining artificial lighting. Until recently, the first method has been the only alternative. Indoor gardeners have used it for some time, especially for flowering and fruiting, and fixtures are available that accommodate both types of bulbs in the same unit. They are somewhat costly and use a greater amount of electricity than the common fixture.

There are so many varying ratios for the fluorescent-incandescent mix that it is difficult to do more than report some of them. Burning 1 incandescent watt to each 5 fluorescent watts has been suggested, as has 1 to 4, 1 to 3 and 1 to 2. One gardener suggests a 1 to 3 ratio when footcandles measure below 1,000, with an increase to a 1 to 2 ratio above 2,000 f.c. Various formulas also combine particular lamps for best effect. One warm-white type might be combined with one cool-white type, or two cool whites to one deluxe warm white. Or reflectorized incandescents might provide the red, while cool white comes up with blue.

Plant growth lamps. The second and easier method is to use wide-spectrum plant growth lamps. These bulbs come close to providing all of the wavelengths that occur in natural daylight, and in the proper proportions. Here, then, is sunlight in a tube.

Plant growth lamps are modified fluorescent lamps and are sold under the trademarks of Gro-Lux, Plant-Gro and Plant-Light, among others. Since the green and yellow parts of the spectrum have no known influence on a plant's biological functions, special fluorescent phosphor lamps were developed that minimize these rays and concentrate instead on emitting the blue and red rays

Type	Wattages	Hours	Length	Diameter	Pins
Incandescent					
General Household Lamps	15, 25, 40, 50, 60, 75, 100, 150, 200, 500	750-1,000			
Reflector Flood-lights and Spotlights	30, 50, 75, 150	1,000			
Parabolic Reflec-torized (PAR)	75, 150	1,000			
Cool Beam Flood Lamps	75, 150, 300	1,000			
PS-30 Reflectorized Bulbs (PS)	150, 250	1,000			
Lumiline Tubes	30, 40, 60	1,000			
Showcase Bulbs	25-75	1,000			
Plant Life	75, 150	1,000			
Fluorescent					
Standard Preheat	4-90	6,000-22,500	6"-60"	5/8"-2 1/8"	bi-pin
Instant-Start	40	7,500	48"	1 1/2", 2 1/8"	bi-pin
Rapid-Start	30, 34, 40	18,000-34,000	36", 48"	1 1/2"	bi-pin
Instant-Start Slim Line	20-75	7,500-22,500	42"-96"	3/4"-1 1/2"	single pin
Rapid-Start High Output (HO)	25-110	9,000-22,500	18"-96"	1 1/2"	recessed double contact
Rapid-Start Very High Output (VHO) and Rapid Start Super High Output (SHO)	110-219	9,000-16,000	48", 72" 96"	1 1/2"	recessed double contact
Reflectorized T-12	110, 135, 165, 215	12,000	48", 96"	1 1/2"	recessed double contact
Power Groove and Power Twist	110, 160, 215	9,000	48", 60" 72", 96"	2 1/8"	recessed double contact
Mod-U-Line, U-Bent, Curvalume	40	12,000	24" x 6" 24" x 3 5/8"	1 1/2"	bi-pin
Circline	22, 32, 40	9,000	8 1/4", 12", 16"	1 1/8"	4-pin
Plant growth					
Gro-Lux	8, 14, 15, 20, 30, 40	6,000-20,000	15", 18", 24", 36", 48"	1", 1 1/2"	bi-pin
	73	12,000	96"	1 1/2"	single pin
	105, 110, 160, 215	10,000-12,000	48", 72", 96"	1 1/2"	recessed double contact
Plant-Gro					
Plant-Light	8, 14, 15, 20, 30, 40	6,000-12,000	12"-48"	5/8", 1", 1 1/2"	bi-pin
Agro Lite	15, 20, 40	7,500-20,000	18", 24", 48"	1", 1 1/2"	bi-pin
Gro-Lux Wide Spectrum	40	7,500	48"	1 1/2"	bi-pin
	75	7,500	96"	1 1/2"	single pin
	105, 110, 160, 215	7,500	48", 72", 96"	1 1/2"	recessed double contact
Vita Lite	14, 15, 20, 30, 40	13,000-33,000	12"-48"	5/8", 1", 1 1/2"	bi-pin
	38, 51, 55, 75	13,000-22,000	36", 48", 72"	1 1/2"	single pin
	60, 85, 110, 160, 215	10,000-14,000	72", 96"	1 1/2"	recessed double contact

Many manufacturers offer ready-made étagères especially for plants. This particular model has plant-growth lamps built into the shelves.

needed for healthy plant growth. Because of the missing values the light tends to have a purplish or pinkish cast. This light enhances flower color—reds scream red, pinks become phosphorescent and yellows glow. Foliage appears lusher under "grow lights"—they become a richer dark green than they do under "white" light. This special effect can be exploited in interior decorating, although the intense purplish effect given off by some lamps may sometimes be difficult to deal with. If you find the color offensive, use these special lamps only when the room is not in use and provide alternate lighting when you are at home.

The newer "wide-spectrum" growth tubes include the visible blue and far-red rays, and sometimes ultraviolet rays as well. They not only help plant growth, but also provide truer perception of plant color than the earlier models of plant lights. Gro-Lux Wide Spectrum has a pink colored light that is easier to accommodate to the home environment than some of the lights with darker hues. Due to the added far-red in wide-spectrum bulbs, which is not visible, the light tends to appear about 78 percent as strong as that emitted by cool-white tubes. Trade names for the wide-spectrum bulbs include the Gro-Lux model already mentioned, Vita Lite and Agro Lite.

Fixtures and Equipment

Incandescent sockets are the familiar screw-in type. They should be made of porcelain when lamps larger than 75 watts are used, to insure good contact and to prevent shorting out.

Fluorescent tubes require their own special fixtures. The 2 most common types of fixtures are "industrial," which have a built-in reflector, and "strip" or "channel," which do not. The industrial fixture is made to hang in the open as a means of reflecting light. Indoor gardeners who have large setups commonly use banks of industrial fixtures with reflectors.

The channel fixture is used in constricted places, such as bookcases or cabinets, where the supporting background can be made reflective by painting it white. (Matte white with its textured surface reflects more light than glossy paint with its smooth surface.) Both fixture types are available in units that can accommodate from 1 to 4 tubes.

Lighting fixtures may be installed so that the light source is concealed or obscured. This may be particularly appropriate in the living room or dining room where an exposed fixture might not look very attractive. The disadvantage of this method is that the distance from lamp to plant is fixed and flexibility can then be achieved only by using bulbs of higher or lower wattages.

Temporary clamp-on incandescent sockets with reflectors or a photographer's lamp on a tripod might be alternatives to consider "when company comes," or for semipermanent supplementary illumination during the winter months when the sun is south of the border.

Fluorescent fixtures may also be suspended from chains to allow for the adjustment brought about by plant growth.

For the casual home gardener, who may not be interested in setting up elaborate artificial lighting systems, various pieces of furniture are now sold that provide 2 or 3 trays with fixtures, reflectors and automatic timers built in. Such items are available from some of the plant lighting manufacturers listed on page 139.

A mobile lighted case can be effective used against the wall or as a room divider. See instructions below for construction.

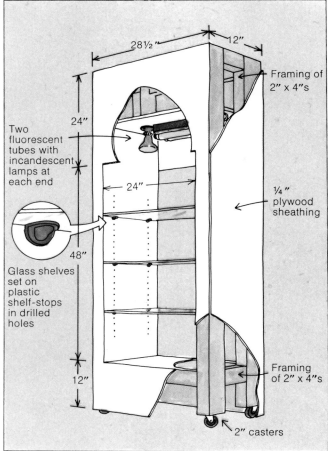

28½"

12"

Framing of 2" x 4"s

24"

Two fluorescent tubes with incandescent lamps at each end

24"

¼" plywood sheathing

48"

Glass shelves set on plastic shelf-stops in drilled holes

12"

Framing of 2" x 4"s

2" casters

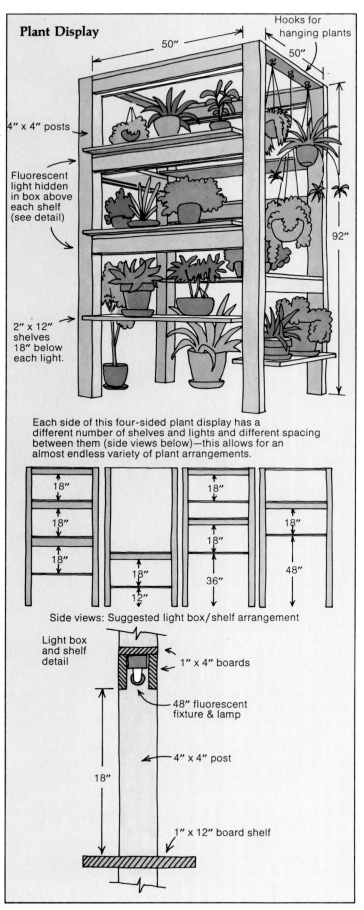

Plant Display

50″

Hooks for hanging plants

50″

4″ x 4″ posts

Fluorescent light hidden in box above each shelf (see detail)

92″

2″ x 12″ shelves 18″ below each light.

Each side of this four-sided plant display has a different number of shelves and lights and different spacing between them (side views below)—this allows for an almost endless variety of plant arrangements.

18″
18″
18″

18″
18″
18″
12″

18″
18″
36″

18″
48″

Side views: Suggested light box/shelf arrangement

Light box and shelf detail

1″ x 4″ boards

48″ fluorescent fixture & lamp

4″ x 4″ post

18″

1″ x 12″ board shelf

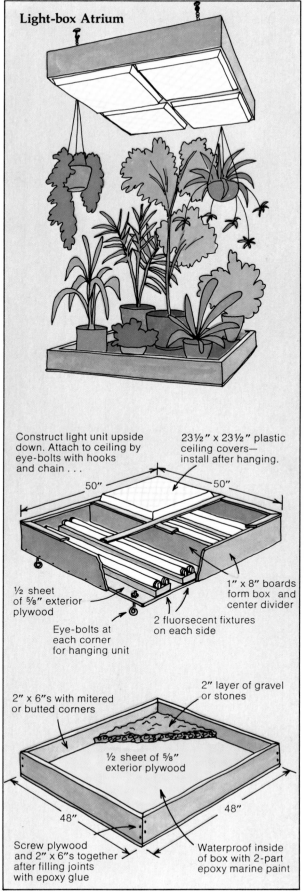

Light-box Atrium

Construct light unit upside down. Attach to ceiling by eye-bolts with hooks and chain . . .

23½″ x 23½″ plastic ceiling covers— install after hanging.

50″

50″

½ sheet of ⅝″ exterior plywood

Eye-bolts at each corner for hanging unit

1″ x 8″ boards form box and center divider

2 fluorescent fixtures on each side

2″ x 6″s with mitered or butted corners

2″ layer of gravel or stones

½ sheet of ⅝″ exterior plywood

48″

48″

Screw plywood and 2″ x 6″s together after filling joints with epoxy glue

Waterproof inside of box with 2-part epoxy marine paint

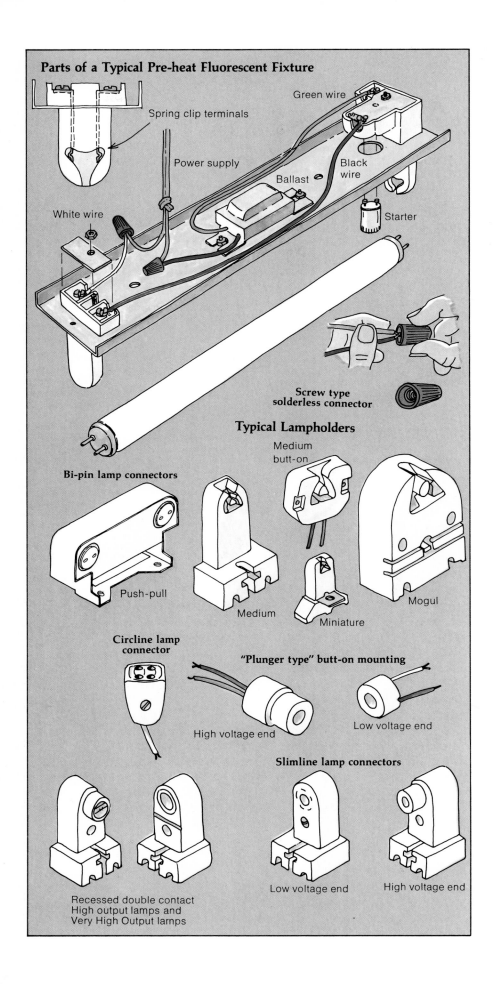

Parts of a Typical Pre-heat Fluorescent Fixture

Green wire

Spring clip terminals

Power supply

Black wire

Ballast

White wire

Starter

Screw type solderless connector

Typical Lampholders

Medium butt-on

Bi-pin lamp connectors

Push-pull

Medium

Miniature

Mogul

Circline lamp connector

"Plunger type" butt-on mounting

High voltage end

Low voltage end

Slimline lamp connectors

Recessed double contact
High output lamps and
Very High Output lamps

Low voltage end

High voltage end

MINIATURE GARDENS

Even the smallest garden contains enough room for the basics of gardening: plants, sunlight, soil, and the rewards only growing plants can give.

You don't have to have a plot of ground or a sunny window to grow a garden. In fact, you can even be bedridden. The answer lies in miniature plants in proportionately small containers. Complete gardens that you can hold in your hands represent the ultimate in gardening pleasure. The only way you can plant and care for them is with intimate contact. You smell the goodness of moist earth and watch the little plants grow: You see the slightest changes, every new leaf, every unfurling bud.

Landscapes in Miniature

When you place a number of different plants in one container you are creating a landscape. This is true whether you are working with a fish tank or bowl, a brandy snifter or terrarium, a bottle or shallow bonsai tray.

Depending on your personal likes, the plants you have available, the container and where you want your landscape to be, you can create a woodland dell, a desert, or a rocky or sandy coastline. You can do your landscaping in the manner of a garden you have visited or seen pictured in Japan, England, the Alps, or even arrange the plants in rows, representing an organized nursery.

Terrarium Plantings

The terrarium was originally invented as a way of transporting living plants from the far parts of the world when voyages took months or even years. Terrariums were carried by Captain Cook on his voyages around the world and by Captain Bligh on the voyage of the Bounty. Today's terrariums are more decorative in nature, but they still allow you to have a garden that can be maintained for long periods of time with a minimum amount of attention.

The most common misconception about terrariums is that they require no care and will thrive just about anywhere you would like to see a little spot of nature. Do not be misled. A terrarium is simply a living microcosm of nature.

Collections of cacti and other succulents need at least a few hours of direct sun to stay shapely. Other plants need bright, indirect light and most will do better with some direct sun, especially early in the morning or late in the afternoon. Terrariums of all kinds, as well as bottle gardens, grow perfectly in a fluorescent-lit garden. They need water from time to time, as well as routine maintenance to remove spent growth and to keep rampant growers compact. A preplanted terrarium that appears to be stuffed with plants is not a good investment; also avoid terrarium kits for growing herbs. Herbs make fine potted plants for a sunny window or under fluorescent lights, but they need fresh, circulating air and perfect drainage. They are not terrarium material.

Air-borne terrariums. Mostly we think of terrariums as tabletop decorations, but they can also be suspended from ceiling hooks or wall brackets. Macramé holders are excellent, and have a natural appearance that is in keeping with

1. Clean and polish bottle with moist paper towel held in wooden tongs. Dampen towel with window-cleaning spray to remove stains. Let dry before planting.

2. Add 1 inch layers of sand and charcoal chips — then a few inches of potting soil using a funnel and paper tube extension to help keep dust down and off sides of bottle.

3. Roll larger, leafy plants in paper cylinder to slip them through the neck without damage.

4. Use wooden tongs to lower small plants through the neck and to maneuver all plants into position.

terrariums. Leaded glass terrariums are on the market, designed for hanging. Some of them are beautifully conceived, with an ornate Wardian (named for the Victorian designer Mr. Ward) look. When you select any glass container, remember that plants will do best in clear rather than tinted glass.

Planting Basics

Most containers used for miniature landscape gardening have no drainage holes. To help keep the growing medium in good health, and therefore sweet smelling and conducive to good growth, first line the bottom of the container with a half inch of charcoal chips. You will find these chips in bags wherever indoor plants and supplies are sold. Next, add a minimum of 1 inch of potting soil. The easiest way is to use a commercially prepared medium labeled "for terrarium plantings." It is true that not all of these mediums are what they are cracked up to be. The most common complaint is that they are too dense, too rich, too moisture retentive. This sounds like three separate faults, but, in fact, they are all interrelated. If your bag of terrarium soil appears to be any of these things, add some vermiculite or perlite. Any of the soilless mixtures are also fine for miniature landscapes (see page 26).

If you are planting a desertscape, using only cacti and other succulents that grow naturally in sandy, dry places, add extra sand, grit or perlite to terrarium soil. Actually, most succulents are not very particular about their growing medium. Unless you water with a heavy hand, there should be no problem. If you want a rocky or mountainous effect, use pieces of lightweight stone, such as featherock. (Check at your garden center.)

6. A spool on a stick can be used to tamp and firm soil.

7. Shaping and pruning can be done with a razor blade taped to a stick. Pick up prunings with tongs.

5. A spoon taped to a stick is great for digging planting holes, positioning plants, covering roots, and shaping the terrain.

8. Use a bulb syringe to wash sides of glass, water roots into place and settle soil. Use it dry to blow dust and soil particules off glass or leaves.

Bottle Planting

Bowls, dishes, brandy snifters and fish tanks are easy to plant and maintain because you can reach your hands into them. Small necked bottles are quite another thing. Like switching on the lights when you know the electricity is off, you will find yourself expecting to use your hands for planting, when actually you will have to use long handled tools.

To place charcoal chips and the growing medium in a bottle, you can fashion a fairly effective funnel from a rolled piece of newspaper. This will help to keep particles of soil off of the inside walls of the bottle. To move the soil around and shape the terrain, you can use a piece of slender bamboo stake with a half-teaspoon measuring spoon taped onto the end.

When you are ready to "bottle" your plants, gently remove most of the soil from the roots. Then drop each plant through the neck and, using your bamboo and spoon spade, coax it into position and cover the roots with soil.

Bottle gardens do best in bright but not direct sunlight. If sun shines directly on the bottle for more than an hour or two, the plants are likely to be cooked. Bottle gardens do superbly under two fluorescent tubes, one cool white, one warm white, of either 20 or 40 watts, burned 12 to 14 hours a day. Add a little water if: the soil in your bottle garden appears to be dry, the plants appear lackluster, no moisture droplets form inside. To remove yellowing leaves, spent flowers or excess growth, tape a single edged razor blade to a piece of slender bamboo and use it as your cutting tool. You can remove clippings with a mechanic's pick-up tool (sold at automobile parts stores) or by manipulating two pieces of bamboo stake, chopstick fashion. It is important that you remove dying leaves and flowers; otherwise they will rot.

FLOWERING HOUSEPLANTS

These are houseplants that almost never stop blooming, plus year-round bulbs and seasonal flowering plants.

Blooming plants will provide you both with blooms to look forward to and the enjoyment of whatever is in bloom at the moment. By selecting several species of blooming plants that come into flower either seasonally or continually, it is possible for you to have plants in containers that flower every day of the year.

In the winter, flowering plants need a few hours of direct sun to bloom well, even the kinds that thrive in shade in the summer. Humidity around flowering plants will help them develop an abundance of full-size flowers.

Phosphorus promotes blooms. A water-soluble fertilizer with high phosphorus content (a 5-10-5 analysis, for example) will hurry otherwise healthy plants into bloom. Use plant food according to package directions. Some growers of African violets and begonias use this analysis or a similar one each month, feeding with a more evenly balanced fertilizer inbetween times (23-21-17, for example).

African Violet

Alphabetically and in popularity, these plants—originally collected in Africa in the late 19th century—come first in a listing of flowering plants. No other plant equals *Saintpaulia* in its ability to thrive and bloom indoors for months on end. With a few plants and proper care it is possible to have continual blooms the year around.

The leaves are velvety, dark green, broad ovals, slightly hairy, on short stalks growing in rosette fashion. Flowers may be single or double, fringed or ruffled, in white or shades of pink, red, violet, purple or blue.

Despite their reputation for being temperamental, African violets are no more difficult to keep than many other container plants. They simply want plenty of light but no burning sun (they can take more in winter), evenly moist soil at all times and good humidity. African violets also thrive under artificial lights (see page 62), making a colorful garden possible even in dark hallways.

Those with plain green leaves are termed "boys," and those with frilly, notched and ruffled leaves, often with a large white area in the center, are called "girls." These terms have nothing to do with the ability of the plants to bloom; both kinds will bloom profusely given good growing conditions.

African violets flower best with only one crown (the area where stems come together and join the roots). New crown growth can be removed and used for rooting new plants.

There are thousands of African violets to choose from. Consult local experts or plant catalogs for the varieties you find most appealing.

Some people grow only the latest hybrids while others are interested in assembling a collection of all the *Saintpaulia* species—the original species from which our modern hybrids have been derived. Variation in size, color and leaf texture offer all manner of choices for specialized collections. With a good selection of plants and proper care it is possible to have some plants in bloom

African violets

Agapanthus

Anthurium

Two of the many flowering begonias:
Semperflorens (top) and Rieger
hybrid (below).

every month of the year. For an impressive display, group blooming plants together in one spot.

Remember, African violets need good filtered light, moisture (see special watering directions on page 27), regular feedings and special, pasteurized soil of equal parts loam, sand and peat moss; we recommend prepackaged special mediums.

Agapanthus

In many parts of the Sun Belt this plant is almost as familiar as the geranium is elsewhere. Unfortunately most gardeners in cold climates don't realize what a fine potted plant it is. Lily of the Nile has evergreen, swordlike leaves and intermittently through the year umbels of blue or white flowers. Dwarf forms in both colors offer further interest for the plant collector. Keep evenly moist and feed regularly. Indoors, give it as much sun as possible; outdoors, either sun or shade is acceptable.

Anthurium

The exotic *Anthurium* or flamingo flower is from the American tropics. It has beautiful heart shaped or lancelike leaves in rich shades of green or variegated with white, some with a rose color underneath. Unfortunately the decorative leaved species have insignificant flowers whereas those with bright flowers have rather plain leaves. Some of the largest and most colorful forms have been developed by growers in Hawaii. The flowers are brilliant oranges and reds or soft greenish or pinkish whites. Most of the color is in the heart shaped spathe surrounding the tiny flowers. All varieties love humidity and warmth.

Begonia

This plant family represents a vast source of beauty for the container gardener. There are miniatures as small as a tea cup, towering plants as large as bushes or even trees and a full range of sizes in between.

The common wax or annual begonia (*Begonia semperflorens*) has a fine, fibrous root system that sends up cupped, roundish leaves set on crisp, fleshy stems, with an endless number of flowers. In fact, *semperflorens* means "everblooming." A basket of these is shown on this page. Best growth and blooms come from seedlings started each year in early winter (page 120); otherwise, take cuttings of stems with branches. Wax begonias come with single, semidouble or fully double flowers.

Sunlight and feedings of fertilizer every other week will keep wax begonias in bloom. Pot in a mixture of equal parts soil, sand and peat moss, or use a soilless, premixed medium. Allow the mixture to dry slightly between waterings.

Angel-wing begonias combine beautiful foliage with clusters of pink, red, orange or white blooms. Their stems are like cane or bamboo stems, swollen at the joints. Kusler hybrids, sold by begonia specialists, are the best.

Some upright, branching begonias defy neat classification. They borrow and combine characteristics from *B. semperflorens*, angel-wing and hairy leafed varieties (page 92). 'Odorata Alba' and 'Tea Rose' even have lightly scented flowers.

Other miscellaneous begonias include excellent, easy-to-grow basket varieties: 'Alpha Gere', 'Marjorie Daw' and the new Rieger hybrids. Be sure to consider also the beef-steak and other rhizomatous begonias. See pages 89 and 92 for further discussion.

Begonias are easy to propogate by division, seed, or leaf cuttings. Friends can exchange bits of their plants and rapidly build an impressive collection of this very variable plant group.

Bird of Paradise

This relative of the banana, known botanically as *Strelitzia reginae*, is one of the most exotic and easiest to grow of all the potted plants. Throughout the year it has showy fans of blue-green leaves. During warm seasons, mature plants send up stalks topped with fascinating birdlike flowers that combine colors of golden orange and peacock blue; these are borne out of green bracts edged with dark red.

Bird of paradise

Calceolaria

These plants have vividly colored pouch shaped flowers that survive from late winter until hot weather kills them. Few growers will go to the trouble it takes to raise them from seeds, which must be planted in a cool, moist place in the spring or summer for blooms to appear the following year. If you receive one as a gift, keep it cool and moist in semisun. The smaller flowered yellow *Calceolaria* seen in nurseries and florists in the winter makes a splendid plant in frost-free winter climates or for a cool greenhouse.

Calceolaria

Christmas Cactus

This perennial favorite is known botanically as *Schlumbergera bridgesii*, a complicated name for a very uncomplicated plant. New hybrids have expanded the choice of flower color (red is the original species) to include white, purple, and orange. Breeding efforts have not only expanded the length of the blooming period but also given a wider range in blooming times. The similar Thanksgiving cactus is called *S. truncata*. Its leaves have two oppositely pointed tips, compared to the smooth edged Christmas cactus leaf ends. Cool nights and short days induce budding in the fall.

Chrysanthemum

Sometimes called "mums" for short, potted ones from a florist will last for days, even weeks longer, if you keep them cool and moist and provide a little sunlight daily. If flower buds are coming, nourish every other week with a plant food. When the plants begin to wither, set them aside in a cool place. Keep the soil barely moist and plant outdoors in early spring. Cut the old stems back to the ground.

Plant chrysanthemums in containers, just as you would in the ground. They can be left outdoors or brought in while in bloom. Chrysanthemums also make showy hanging baskets and can be trained as cascades or standards.

Cineraria

The Canary Islands gave us *Senecio cruentus*, a plant that grows small daisylike flowers in a rainbow of vivid colors that blanket the bright green leaves. Keep florist's plants as cool as possible but in good light, and water freely. If given fertilizer, the buds will continue to open for weeks. Remove old flowers, making way for the buds that are still forming. When buds stop coming, discard the plant.

Chrysanthemum

Cineraria

Christmas cactus

Clivia

Columnea

Crossandra

Easter lily

Clivia

Grandmother's kaffir lily was a *Clivia miniata*, an amaryllis relative with fans of dark, evergreen, leathery leaves. These leaves provide a perfect foil for the strong, upright stems topped with umbels of salmon pink flowers that appear in spring or summer. Several strains and varieties are available in outstanding colors and shapes. Pollinate and reap further reward—the seeds have a bright, cherry red color and stay on for months.

Columnea

There are about 150 different species in this part of the gesneriad family. They come from Central and South America and the West Indies, and their natural habitat is the damp, tropical forest. Columneas make wonderful container plants, adapting well to indoor conditions. Since they are semiupright or trailing plants, they look particularly well in hanging baskets. The brightly colored, tubular flowers come in orange, scarlet and yellow, and will bloom throughout the winter. Flowers range in size from ½ inch to 4 inches, according to the variety. Leaves can be as small as tiny buttons or as long as 3 inches. These plants require semishade and moist air.

Crossandra

This lovely flower, also called the firecracker flower, belongs to the acanthus family and comes from India. Seldom growing higher than 1 foot when kept indoors in a container, it has glossy, green leaves and tubular, orange flowers that expand at the top and bloom almost continuously. It needs a warm atmosphere and must be kept evenly moist but never sodden. Grow it in a mixture of half peat moss and half potting soil. It flourishes under fluorescent lighting.

Cyclamen

A thick leaved plant of silvery green, with translucent stems and veins, *Cyclamen persicum* provides showy butterflylike blossoms in white and shades of pale pink through vivid red, some ruffled and variegated.

Cyclamen from florists are often received as gifts. Most people prefer to discard a *Cyclamen* after its blooming season, but you may like to try to keep yours. Place in semisun, away from drafts, and keep the soil moist at all times, watering from below to keep the foliage dry. New buds can be encouraged by applying liquid fertilizer every two or three weeks.

After the flowers cease to come, try to keep the leaves growing well. This will maintain the health of the tuber that will send up next year's flowers. In early summer, allow the bulbs to enter a dormancy period.

Easter Lily

Lilies grow well in containers, and the fragrant white *Lilium longiflorum* is a favorite. Keep plants from florists moist and provided with some sunlight. Cut off the flowers as they wither, but allow foliage to continue growing, thus storing energy in the bulb. Pots can be placed outdoors and will often produce a second bloom in a single season.

Cyclamen

Flame Violet

The *Episcia* is a relative of the African violet. It is grown primarily for its beautiful foliage, but whenever days are sunny and the air warm and humid, it will put on a festive show of scarlet, yellow or blue flowers. *Episcia reptans*, the flame violet, started the popular trend of growing these tropical beauties.

Although attractive in regular flower pots, episcias are at their best in hanging baskets because, like strawberries, they have "runners" or stolons that cascade gracefully from the mother plant.

Episcias resent cold weather; they like humidity, but will tolerate the dryness of the average house if the soil is kept evenly moist.

Flame violet

Geranium

These South African plants appeal to almost everyone. And they are so versatile! If you like to collect plants, then geraniums are for you; there are thousands of species and named varieties, each slightly different from the others. Cheerful red or pink geraniums have convinced many people that they would like to try their hand at container gardening—and because of this same charm, interior decorators find geraniums irresistible, if a bit difficult to handle where sunlight isn't abundant.

Common geraniums are hybrids of *Pelargonium hortorum*, often called zonale because of the dark green or blackish zone in each leaf. Varieties are available in red, pink, apricot, tangerine, salmon and white.

Dwarf geraniums stay under 8 inches in height and will grow for many months, even years, in a 2 to 4-inch pot.

Fancy-leaf geraniums belong in the same classification as common kinds. They have varicolored leaves, often in beautiful bronzes, scarlets and creamy yellows.

Geranium

Ivy geraniums, cultivars of *Pelargonium peltatum*, bear leathery leaves with a shape uncannily like that of English ivy, to which they are in no way related. They excel in hanging baskets, but need full sun indoors as well as a moist, cool atmosphere. The flowers, often veined with a darker shade of their color, come in showy clusters, sometimes nearly smothering the plant.

There are all kinds of geranium oddities. There is a group with prickly stems, called a cactus geranium. *Pelargonium* 'Poinsettia' may have quilled and squarish red or pink petals. 'Jeanenne' has single, salmon colored flowers that are pinked along the edges like Sweet Williams. There are also bird's egg, New Life, phlox and rosebud geraniums, climbing kinds and many more.

Hydrangea

Hydrangea

Potted hydrangeas are varieties of *Hydrangea macrophylla*, a Japanese plant. Those received as gifts need abundant moisture to keep the foliage and flowers in good condition; if the soil dries out, they will wilt badly. The flower buds form during one summer for the following year's blooms. Temperatures below 25°F will kill the buds.

Impatiens

These are sometimes called sultanas or patience plants. The plants most commonly grown today are hybrids of *Impatiens sultanii* and *I. holstii*. Many outstanding varieties are easily grown from seeds sown in warm moist soil in early spring. These low-growing plants have small, flat flowers that literally cover the dark green, maroon or variegated green and white leaves. *Impatiens* thrives in shaded areas outdoors, but needs some sunlight and moist air in the house.

Impatiens

Jerusalem cherry

King's crown

Lipstick vine

Phalaenopsis orchid

Passion flower

Jerusalem or Christmas Cherry

This colorful relative of the eggplant and potato is named *Solanum pseudocapsicum*. It has small leaves and white flowers and produces red or yellow round fruits. Provide coolness and lots of moisture. Cut back drastically after the fruiting season. Place outdoors during warm weather in a shady spot. The proper culture can produce a large, woody shrub. The fruit is not edible.

King's Crown

Jacobinia carnea, shown here, is a bushy tropical plant with pink flowers and corrugated dark green leaves. There is also a variety with tangerine flowers. It is best grown from tip cuttings started in the winter for summer bloom, in the summer for winter flowers. Treat the same as for geraniums, but with a little more moisture.

Lipstick Vine

In a sunny eastern window or in similar light outdoors (in warm weather) this is a superb basket plant. *Aeschynanthus radicans* has waxy leaves on stems that grow up to 2 feet long. Off and on throughout the year, clusters of buds form at the ends of these leaves, each fuzzy red flower bud nestled in a maroon brown calyx—hence, the name lipstick vine. It grows well in a soilless medium that is kept moist.

Orchid

A collection of orchids will provide blooms the year around, and there are many that will thrive in a window garden or under fluorescent lights. If you would like to experiment with orchids, start with the cattleya, clamshell, butterfly, dancing lady or lady slipper. Study catalogs from orchid growers and read books on their culture. Orchid growing is challenging but rewarding.

Oxalis

These plants have cloverlike leaves that fold tightly together at dusk and open again each morning. Even those grown under fluorescent lights fold up at sundown. Many kinds make outstanding potted plants and elegant subjects for hanging baskets. Grand Duchess (*Oxalis variabilis*) has large white, pink or rose colored flowers. Bermuda buttercup (*O. cernua* and its double flowered form) has yellow, fragrant flowers. *O. rubra* has pink flowers. *O. ortgiesii* is a tree that grows to 24 inches, with yellow flowers. *O. deppei* has pink flowers and is called lucky clover. These plants like sun and moisture, except during dormant periods.

Passion Flower

This vine is grown for its fascinating flowers. *Passiflora alato-caerulea* (sometimes called *P. pfordtii*) grows a beautiful flower that combines colors of creamy white, pink and blue. Red flowered *P. coccinea* will bloom well throughout both winter and spring in a sunny location indoors. This rapid-growing vine likes a moist, sunny environment and must have something on which to attach its tendrils. Try a trellis or ceiling-to-floor pole, or use twine and train it to frame a window.

Oxalis

Poinsettia

Poinsettia

Of Mexican origin, *Euphorbia pulcherrima* should be kept out of drafts in a warm place, and soil should be evenly moist. After the colorful bracts (we think of them as flowers) fall, set the plant in a cool room and let the soil stay nearly dry until the spring. Then move to a sunny spot, water well and watch for new growth. Repot in new soil and cut back the canes to 6 inches from the pot rim. Poinsettias can be grown in a sunny interior or a protected area outdoors. Pinching encourages more branches and thus more blooms. Bring indoors in autumn when nights begin to cool. Keep in absolute darkness from sundown to sunup for 10 weeks beginning in October to assure holiday blooms.

Miniature rose

Rose, Miniature

These plants are perfect copies in miniature of the foliage and blooms of the outdoor hybrid tea, floribunda or moss roses. They are available in an assortment of colors, and by careful pruning, are easily kept under 12 inches in overall height. Flowering will occur with moderate warmth (62 to 72°F), at least 4 hours direct sunlight daily, and moist, fresh air. They will also thrive under artificial lighting (see page 62). Buy potted miniature roses from garden centers or any mail-order rose specialist.

Shrimp Plant

The curious bracts of this plant, *Justicia brandegeana*, formerly called *Beloperone guttata*, remind many people of shrimp. The bracts bear small white flowers, typical of the mint family. After the flowers are gone, the bracts remain for weeks, and it is quite usual for this plant to be in bloom constantly. The original species has pinkish bronze bracts; 'Yellow Queen' is chartreuse. Both are good for pots and hanging baskets. Put them in a sunny place and keep their soil on the dry side.

Shrimp plant

Tulbaghia

This perennial from South Africa belongs to the lily family. *Tulbaghia fragrans*, from the Transvaal, sometimes called pink agapanthus, is an especially attractive variety. It has a slender stalk that grows up to 18 inches high, which is crowned with a cluster of small, lavender pink, fragrant flowers. These will bloom all through the winter months. This plant does well indoors with cool temperatures and some fresh air.

Zebra Plant

Aphelandra, of the acanthus family, is a tropical evergreen that has been recently added to the list of indoor plants now available. *Aphelandra* has dark leaves with striking, light colored veins, which explains its common name. Of all the species, *A. squarrosa* 'Louisae' from Brazil is the most spectacular. It has spikes of waxy bright yellow bracts and white flowers rising above emerald green leaves, and other species have bracts that are red or orange. It is not an easy plant to keep blooming outside a greenhouse; it needs a lot of light and moist air to encourage flower growth. Be sure the soil is always kept damp. Pot in a standard mix but with double the amount of peat moss. After flowering, cut the stems back so that the lower leaves will drop off, giving the plant a leggy appearance. Feed with weak liquid fertilizer every two weeks in the summer.

Tulbaghia

Zebra plant

Bulbs as Houseplants

All plants grow in a cycle, which includes a resting period. With many foliage and flowering container plants, this is hardly noticeable, but the bulbs discussed in this section require a real rest—a season of dormancy when the tired, spent top growth dies to the ground and is cut off, and the underground portion is kept dry or barely moist in a cool but frost-free, dark storage place.

In the descriptions that follow, you will find specific instructions for each kind of bulb. One of the nicest rewards in growing bulbs is that each one grows larger—or multiplies—every year. (The term bulbs is used loosely to include corms and tubers as well as true bulbs.)

In their native haunts, growth and dormancy are triggered by naturally rainy and dry seasons. When we tame these wildlings and turn them into sophisticated hybrids, we must also take the responsibility for playing the role of Mother Nature in nurturing the perfect seasonal cycle from sprouting to sprouting.

Most bulbs flowers are not particularly sensitive to day length, which means you can start the growth cycle at any time you can provide suitable temperature, light and moisture. Achimenes and tuberous begonias require the naturally long days of summer to bloom well. In fact, when nights grow longer in early fall, tuberous begonias actively produce seed-bearing female flowers and fewer showy male flowers. And, while caladiums are grown entirely for their beautiful foliage, they too begin to spend energy producing flowers—at the expense of new leaves—at summer's end.

While anemones, ranunculus and freesias care how long the day is, they cannot tolerate hot weather, especially warm nights. In cool but frost-free winter climates, they are as easily cultivated outdoors in pots or ground soil as gladioli are. In the north they require special care—either a cool, sunny, airy, moist greenhouse or plant room, or a fluorescent-lit area that has cool, fresh air.

Achimenes

Amaryllis hybrids

Achimenes

These African violet and gloxinia relatives grow from inch-long, catkinlike scaly rhizomes. Today's hybrids have single or double petunialike flowers in all shades of blue, purple, red, orange, pink and white, often with a contrasting color on the flower face. For color in the shade in summer, achimenes have no equal except for impatiens. They do well in hanging baskets. In early spring, plant the rhizomes 1 inch deep in a soilless mix (Jiffy Mix, for example). Keep warm and moist. Pinch out tip growth a time or two to induce branching. Give some direct sun in the spring, bright shade in the summer. Never let the soil dry out. In the autumn, withhold water. Store rhizomes in dry vermiculite.

Amaryllis

These are among the easiest, most dependable plants for blooming indoors. Their interesting growing cycle is simple to handle. Under good growing conditions, every four leaves will store up a flower bud inside the bulb. Nearly all of the plants are more correctly referred to as the genus *Hippeastrum* but the name *Amaryllis* is so firmly established that it will continue to be used. Inexpensive American hybrids come in white and various shades of red, scarlet and pink, as well as white marked with red or pink. Named Dutch hybrids, often costly, are magnificent in size and color purity. The latest on the scene are the South African hybrids, which often bloom naturally between Thanksgiving and Christmas.

To promote luxuriant leaf growth and the formation of next season's flower buds, provide several hours of sun or bright light all day, along with average house warmth. Keep evenly moist at all times and feed every other week, except in the autumn. Then dry out for at least two months, removing leaves when they dry up. Keep in a cool, dry, dark place. When buds show, or after two or three months' rest, repot and start into growth. Mealybugs are a bad amaryllis pest, especially when they get down into the neck of the bulb.

Anemone

The poppylike flower *Anemone coronaria* is a successful greenhouse plant. It can be grown in containers outdoors in California and Florida; it grows well inside only if it can be kept cool (55°F at night) and humid. Anemones are known for their vivid hues of red, purple, pink and blue. They also grow in white and pastel colors. Soak the tiny corms in water overnight before planting. Keep them cool, dark and slightly moist until evidence of growth appears. Place in an airy, sunny spot indoors or in a partially shaded area outdoors. Water freely and fertilize every other week. Anemones are susceptible to aphids. Store while dormant in a cool, dry place until time for the new cycle.

Caladium

These are showy foliage plants that grow from a fleshy tuber. They are sometimes forced into growth in winter, but do best in warm summer temperatures and a moist atmosphere. Standard varieties are available at most plant stores and mail-order outlets in late winter and spring. Beautiful new hybrids are a good buy.

While caladiums like warmth and humidity, they also thrive in dappled sun or in bright, open shade in the summer. Keep moist at all times. Fertilize every other week from spring until early fall with a well-balanced plant food. In late fall, dry out caladium plants by withholding water, then store the tubers in a warm place (60°F) until spring. Wet soil during dormancy may cause rot.

Calla Lily

The elegant white *Zantedeschia aethiopica* blooms in winter or spring. Plant tubers in late summer. *Z. elliottiana*, with yellow flowers and silver markings on the leaves, and the new pastel hybrids, are summer bloomers. Start these tubers in late winter or early spring. Callas grow best in a sunny area. During the dormant period, keep barely moist. When evidence of growth appears, water freely. After blooms stop and leaves turn yellow, stop watering and feeding. Rest until next season.

Fragrant Gladiolus

This is the common name for *Acidanthera*, an African bulb with gladiolus foliage and fragrant white flowers that are blotched with maroon. Three to six flowers grow on a stalk. Plant new corms in the spring. Keep pots in a sunny location and water freely. Store away for the winter in a cool dry place. Can also be given the same treatment as freesias.

Freesia

South African in origin, these plants grow from small corms planted an inch deep. Foliage is thin, sword shaped. Very fragrant flowers, in shades of yellow, lavender, orange, and white, cluster at the end of slender stems. New corms should be planted in the fall for blooms in late winter or early spring. During their growing season freesias should have sunlight, cool temperatures, moist atmosphere and soil, and feedings every other week. Freesias make excellent subjects for greenhouse culture. After flowers stop being produced and leaves begin to brown, cut watering to dry out corms. Store corms in cool, dry place until the following season.

Anemone

Caladiums

Calla lily

Freesia

Gloriosas

Gloxinias

Gloriosa

The glory lily is also called the climbing lily because of the way in which it climbs by means of tendrillike leaf tips. Flowers have narrow petals that curve backwards. *Gloriosa rothschildiana* produces crimson and yellow flowers. *G. simplex* is a dwarf with flowers that range from yellow to orange according to the amount of sunlight received. *G. superba* climbs up to 10 feet and has yellow flowers that turn red with maturity.

Gloriosa grows best on a trellis or wire mesh. By varying planting times, you can have blooms throughout the year indoors. Give it good moisture and sun during growing season. Rest when dormant until new growth is seen. Its long roots, like those of a large white radish, require a large pot or basket. The tuberous roots are very brittle, so handle them with care when potting.

Gloxinia

These velvety leaved Brazilian plants are members of the gesneriad family. They are known botanically as *Sinningia*. In practice, growers tend to call the natural species sinningias and the hybrids gloxinias. Some miniatures—both hybrids and natural species—have ½-inch leaves and produce inch-long flowers almost constantly. Hybrid gloxinias are available today in many colors in countless combinations, including petals banded with contrasting color and solid-color petals that are heavily spotted or misted with another color. Some are double.

Gloxinias need humidity, along with full sun in the winter and shade in the summer, in order to grow and bloom. Pot the tubers, whenever available, about ½-inch deep. Keep evenly moist at all times. After blooming ceases and leaf growth seems to have reached a standstill, gradually withhold water until stems and leaves die down. Then put the pot and its contents in a cool, dark, mouseproof place for 2 to 4 months while the tuber rests. During this time, keep the soil just barely moist so that the tuber won't shrivel. When the resting period is over, repot into fresh soil, move to light and warmth, provide moisture. Feed growing gloxinias every other week.

Haemanthus

Umbels of tightly packed flowers are sent up by this interesting South African bulb. Foliage is green, much like the amaryllis. It is very longlasting and requires only a short period of dormancy. The plant should receive semisunny light and stay evenly moist, except during the fall and winter rest when it should stay almost dry. Bulbs should not be repotted each year. After their winter rest, begin the water and light cycle again. *Haemanthus albiflos* bears white flowers during June. *H. coccineus* blooms dark red. Salmon-red flowers are borne on *H. katherinae*, and *H. multiflorus* produes dark crimson flowers. All of the red-flowered species are commonly called blood lilies.

Ixia

South Africa gives us another exotic blooming bulb called corn lily. Tall, wiry, yet strong stems produce 6 or more bell-shaped flowers on a dense spike in red, violet, pink, yellow or white, with dark centers. Foliage is grasslike. Ixia needs full sun and lots of water during growing season. See *Freesia* for similar cycle and culture.

Montbretia

This member of the iris family is known botanically as *Crocosmia × crocosmiiflora*. It produces a dense cluster of sword shaped leaves. Tall flower spikes, usually branching, bear orange-red, starlike blooms. Plant pots of corms in a sunny location; treat them like fragrant gladiolus. Store corms in peat moss for the winter.

Ixia

Oxalis

Some species of this family grow from tubers or rhizomes, such as *O. brazili-ensis*, sold as shamrocks by florists. Rosy colored flowers appear above bright green leaves. Many colors and variegations of leaves and flowers are available. *Oxalis* can bloom at different times, depending on the species. Keep moist during growth. Dry off to induce dormancy after leaves fade (see page 84).

Ranunculus

These most beautiful of all buttercups produce an array of double flowers in pink, yellow, orange, red and white. Indoors or outdoors they cannot tolerate dry heat. They also require a frost-free environment. For winter bloom, keep them in a greenhouse or plant room where it is sunny, cool, moist and airy. Plant tubers in the autumn, which is also the time to plant for winter-spring bloom outdoors in mild climates. Aphids find young ranunculus leaves irresistible; spray to control these pests or flowering will be impaired. While in active growth, feed every other week. When flowering stops, dry out, discard tops, remove tubers from the soil and store in dry peat moss or vermiculite in a frost-free place.

Ranunculus

Tuberous Begonia

These showy plants are the mockingbirds of the plant kingdom: Their flowers resemble carnations, roses, daffodils and camellias. All are spectacular plants for decorating a semishady terrace, patio or garden in the summer and early fall. They like a moist soil with plenty of humus; warm days; cool, moist nights and protection from hot, dry winds. For equal flower beauty indoors in the winter, grow the Rieger hybrid begonias. See also pages 80 and 92.

Plant sprouted tubers ½-inch deep in moist, coarse leaf mold, fir bark, or peat moss and sand. Keep them evenly moist at all times, but never soggy wet. Keep warm (70 to 75°F). Tubers are usually ready for planting from February to April. After they form a good root system, pot them in a mixture of equal parts soil, sand, peat moss and leaf mold; keep evenly moist at all times. Fertilizer applied every other week throughout the growing season, until early fall, will encourage steady, vigorous growth. Before frost is expected, bring the plants inside to a warm, dry place. Withhold water until tops die; discard the old leaves and stems, but leave the tubers in the soil. Apply a limited amount of water throughout the dormant period to keep the soil barely damp.

Tuberous begonias

FOLIAGE HOUSEPLANTS

Select colorful desert or rain forest foliages, but remember green is also a color in many shades, textures and forms.

Unlike most flowering plants—which are at peak beauty for only short periods—foliage plants are handsome the year around. You will find unlimited variety in sizes, shapes, leaf patterns and colors.

Nature provides a mind-boggling range of colors in limitless combinations. The variety of textures available in green, variegated and unusual colors can be compared to a fabric store or grandmother's patchwork quilt.

A collection of container plants can be a veritable rain forest of humidity loving tropicals or an arid desert of sun-worshipping cacti and other succulents. Perhaps the most pleasing garden is a blending of compatible plants from many habitats, so that a number of contrasts can be achieved. Select plants that you like—that you will be happy caring for, and that require growing conditions suitable to your environment.

Most of the plants identified in this chapter are durable, easily cultivated kinds that can stand a wide range of temperatures, moisture and lighting conditions. Failure with foliage plants comes most often from careless watering practices—either too much or too little. Remember, with the exception of a few cacti, no plant can exist in dry, bricklike soil. Likewise, constant saturation pleases only a few plants. See watering directions, along with other basics of container gardening, beginning on page 22.

Select top-quality plants from reliable sources where you can be reasonably sure they are free from disease. Consider the joy of starting new plants from seeds, cuttings, air layering or divisions.

Acorus

If you want a bit of white and green variegated grass to complete a planting arrangement, consider *Acorus gramineus.* It forms a grassy spray about 10 inches tall. *A. gramineus* 'Pusillus' is a miniature form with leaf fans 3 inches tall. *A. calamus* 'Variegatus' is called sweet flag. It, too, has beautifully variegated foliage, flat and similar to an iris. All of these like to have a soil that is constantly wet.

Asparagus Fern

Vegetable asparagus has many relatives that make good container plants. African in origin, these members of the lily family are reliable growers, to be enjoyed in indoor or outdoor shady gardens. The feathery cool green branchlets grow on stalks that reach lengths of from 1 to 6 feet and are handsome trained on string or wire or in hanging baskets.

Asparagus setaceus (known until recently as *A. plumosus*) is the lacy "fern" often used by florists with roses. Its semiclimbing stems have prickles and may form purple berries. Preferring an outdoor environment, it does not do well as a houseplant. *A. densiflorus* 'Sprengeri' has coarser leaves than those of the vegetable. It is a durable plant that can live through drought, but loves hu-

Acorus

Asparagus fern

Aspidistra

Begonias

midity. Its branchlets are set with ½-inch needlelike leaves and some thorns. Fragrant, tiny white summer flowers are followed by cherry red berries around Christmastime. *A. asparagoides* 'Myrtifolius', with broad rather than needlelike leaves, is another species cultivated by indoor gardeners. Florists call it baby smilax, and use it in floral arrangements. *A. densiflorus* 'Myers' is a relatively new addition to container plants. It forms spears shaped like a bottle brush that reach as high as 18 inches. *A. macowanii* (sometimes called *A. myriocladus*) grows, shrublike, to as high as 6 feet, with linear leaves, greenish white flowers and reddish berries.

All *Asparagus* species do best with very high light intensity. This is one plant that won't compromise on light. Gardeners who have grown asparagus ferns successfully outdoors are often tempted to bring them indoors only to be surprised in a matter of a few days as extraordinarily long (6 feet and longer) stems reach out to find the light they need. If you don't have a really bright spot it may be best to pass this plant by.

Aspidistra

Aspidistra is common in the South, usually growing as a completely carefree—and therefore neglected—groundcover in dense, dark shade. Its common name of "cast-iron plant" is a direct commentary on how sturdy and tolerant this plant really is. The fact that *Aspidistra* was a favorite indoor plant during the Victorian era when houses were anything but bright and airy serves as an additional testimonial to the toughness of this plant. Patience is the prime requirement needed by owners of small plants; it takes considerable time to grow an *Aspidistra* to specimen size. Ironically, like many "folk" plants, it is not always available in nurseries. This is partly because it grows so slowly and partly because it is not properly appreciated. As a bushy potted plant, 12 to 24 inches tall and wide, the *Aspidistra* simply has no equal when it comes to tolerance of dim light and neglect. Wet or dry, in sun or darkest shade, here's a real toughie to build your confidence as a plant grower indoors or outdoors. *Aspidistra elatior* has cornlike, shiny, dark green leaves that grow to 24 inches long; it occasionally produces purple-brown small flowers near the base of the plant. Its variegated form is shown here. The white markings help to light up a dark corner, rather like sun filtering through a shade tree. A dwarf form, known as *A. minor*, has white spotted black-green leaves. Try to acquire all 3, then display them in attractive pottery containers.

Begonia

This huge and varied family is divided into 3 categories; tuberous rooted, fibrous rooted and ornamental leaf begonias (usually rhizomatous). The tuberous rooted and most of the fibrous rooted begonias are grown for their flowers and are discussed on pages 80 and 89. The plants discussed here are treasured for their leaves.

Hairy leafed begonias have fuzzy textured leaves, and some are splashed with red or silver or various green backgrounds. Try growing *Begonia alleryi*, *B.* 'Mrs. Fred D. Scripps' or *B. drostii*. Beefsteak or star begonias range in size from miniatures to giants and in color from silver to brown. Some are thickly succulent, are often ruffled or have smooth starlike leaves. Favorites include 'Cleopatra', 'Texas Star', 'Silver Star' and 'Maphil'.

Rex begonias come in a variety of rich textures, patterns and colors. While the foliage plant coleus is often likened to a Persian carpet, rex begonias are more like a fine Aubusson. 'Merry Christmas' is the most popular named variety, but there are hundreds of others. It is fun to collect as many different ones as you can find. The stems are densely covered with glistening hairs. Some are tea-cup size, others are as big as a bushel basket. The rexes thrive in warmth, high humidity and bright light, but with little direct sun. They also grow excellently in fluorescent-lit gardens.

An easy-to-grow rhizomatous begonia that looks like a rex, but isn't, is *B. masoniana*, also called iron cross because its leaves are marked with a cross.

Brassaia/Schefflera

Classified as *Schefflera* until recently, these beautiful evergreen tropical foliage plants are now separated into two different genera.

Schefflera digitata and *Brassaia actinophylla*—two popular species—make graceful, durable plants for pots and planters, ranging in size from 5-inch seedlings to trees 6 feet or more tall. Six to eight shiny green, pointed oval leaves grow at the ends of long branches. Clusters of small flowers may be produced.

The recently introduced dwarf schefflera (*S. arboricola*) has smaller leaves and will remain under 2 feet in height if kept in a smaller pot.

All scheffleras are good plants for well-lighted, nonsunny areas, either indoors or on the patio in the summer. Hardiness and choice of scale make them favorites with designers and decorators for commercial spaces and private dwellings, as shown in the 2-level foyer in the photograph above.

This 2-level, skylighted foyer of a city townhouse boasts 2 large specimen trees— a mature *Dizygotheca elegantissima* in the left foreground and *Brassaia actinophylla* in the upper right. Ferns, other foliage plants and blooming species are used throughout the space.

Bromeliads

Columbus discovered pineapples growing on the West Indian island of Guadeloupe on his second voyage to the New World in 1493, but it was not until around 1950 that we began to appreciate the entire pineapple family, the bromeliads. Showy, colorful, even bizarre, they share the edible pineapple's habit of growing a rosette of stiff leathery leaves.

In frost-free climates, bromeliads can be grown outdoors the year around, in pots on the ground, or hanging from and perching in trees. For remarkably beautiful foliage, flowers and long-lasting bracts and berries, they have no equal among other houseplants. Indoors, they grow in sun or shade, do well in fluorescent-lit gardens and look marvelous in wall mounted containers. There are fist-size miniatures and arm-span giants.

Many bromeliads are formed of a rosette of leaves with a cuplike empty area (the "vase") in their center. It is important that the vase always be filled with water. It is a good idea to empty the rosette of water each time before adding more.

The plants should be grown in a coarse, open growing medium, because most bromeliads are air plants in their native haunts. Pot in a mixture of equal parts peat moss and sand, or in unshredded sphagnum moss or in osmunda fiber. Whichever medium you choose, keep it on the dry side; pay more attention to keeping the rosettes of leaves filled with water.

Aechmea. This living vase plant has outstanding foliage all year long, plus showy spikes of pink bracts with blue flowers in season, which are followed by long-lasting scarlet berries. The common name refers to the long, slender tube from which the flower stem grows. In bloom, the plant appears to have provided its own vase because the tube of leaves will hold water.

Ananas. This is the commercial pineapple, which grows with narrow, sharp-edged, gray-green leaves. Sprout your own plant from the cut off top portion of a grocery store pineapple. Allow the cut to dry for several days, and then plant in damp soil. There is a dwarf variety on the market and also one with variegated leaves. Fruits sprout from the middle of the leaf rosette.

Billbergia. *Billbergia nutans*, called queen's tears, is widely grown and easy to obtain. Its rosettes are similar to those of a young pineapple top, except that they are longer and more slender. The pendant, graceful flowers have violet edged, green petals.

Cryptanthus. This plant stays within a few inches from the ground. In fact, their rosettes of leaves stay on such a horizontal plane that as a group they are called "earth stars." Small ones make good terrarium specimens.

Guzmania. This bromeliad forms long yellowish leaves striped with dark red. It produces many red, white or yellow flowers in the winter. Try *Guzmania berteroniana* and *G. zahnii*.

Neoregelia. These bromeliads produce their flowers just above the water in the "vase." The area around the vase on a *Neoregelia* is rosy red and surrounds the tiny blue flowers. Leaves are green with stripes of yellow, white and rose.

Tillandsia. *Tillandsia lindenii* grows as a dark green rosette of narrow long leaves and produces an ornamental spike of bright pink bracts on which splendid blue flowers bloom.

Vriesea. This plant has wide leaves in rosette form. *Vriesea splendens* is zebra striped in brown and produces a tall flamelike bract of orange. A small variety is *V. carinata*; it has brilliant yellow, red and green bracts and tiny short-lived yellow flowers.

Chinese Evergreen

This is the popular name for *Aglaonema modestum*, a durable foliage plant that will grow for long periods of time in plain water. In plant stores you will find

Bromeliads. Top: *Aechmea* species.
Below: *Aechmea recurvata;*

Chlorophytum comosum 'Picturatum'

More bromeliads: **1.** *Neoregelia carolinae*.
2. *Guzmania lingulata* and **3.** the bloom of
Aechmea fasciata.

other aglaonemas with silver and green leaves, which prefer soil culture. All grow amazingly well in dimly lit places. They produce long-lasting red berries.

Chlorophytum

For its fountains of new plantlets that create an airy, graceful appearance, this plant gets its most known common name, the spider plant. Another popular name, the airplane plant, comes from the fact that these plantlets are born in the air, while in most other plant families the babies sprout from seeds. The common spider plant is *Chlorophytum comosum* 'Vittatum'. Other good kinds include *C. comosum* 'Picturatum', which has large, creamy bands down leaf centers, and *C. comosum* 'Mandaianum', which has green leaves edged in creamy white.

Cissus

These members of the grape family are ideal for containers; their vines will spill out of hanging baskets or cascade from pots placed on pedestals or shelves. Or if you like, allow the tendrils to attach themselves to string or trellis. These plants withstand neglect and poor conditions, making them good office or city inhabitants. Overwatering them and moving them around may cause their leaves to fall off.

Cissus antarctica, known as the kangaroo vine because it grows by leaps and bounds, has elongated, shiny green leaves. *C. capensis* (more correctly *Rhoicissus capensis*) has leaves shaped similar to the oak's. *C. rhombifolia* is the popular grape ivy, with dark green leaves formed of three leaflets. *C. discolor*, the group's most showy member, has rosy stems and green leaves flushed with silvery rose.

Chinese evergreen

Cissus

Coleus

Cyperus

Dizygotheca

Dieffenbachia

Fatsia

Coleus

So richly colored are the leaves of this member of the mint family (square stems are the clue) that some people simply call it "foliage." Keep growth tips pinched to promote compact branching. It is easy and fun to grow coleus as a bush or little tree. Spikes of pale blue flowers should be pinched back.

Cyperus

These graceful plants look like something that should be growing by the Nile River. And they do love moisture; keep the pots in saucers of water. *Cyperus papyrus*, the Egyptian paper plant, has umbrellas of grassy leaves that burst out of 3 to 10-foot triangular stems. *C. alternifolius* is smaller, *C. albostriatus* (formerly called *C. elegans*) more delicate. *Cyperus* has a unique appearance, whether grown indoors or out.

Dieffenbachia

Touched to the tongue, the sap from the canelike stems of this plant can cause temporary speechlessness, hence the term dumb cane and references to it as the mother-in-law plant. In large containers dieffenbachias have few equals as accent plants—indoors all year long, or outdoors in warm weather. They are shrubby with thick stems and large, wide, oblong leaves. Modern cultivars offer a choice of tree-like single stem forms, basal-branching forms, and clustering forms that fill a pot with many stems. Dieffenbachias combine many marbled shades of green, chartreuse, cream and white. Mature plants will reach the ceiling and will need air layering to eliminate ugly, gawky stems (see page 125). All kinds adapt well to indoor living spaces. They contrast pleasingly with cornlike dracaenas, spathiphyllums and ferns.

Dizygotheca

False aralia is another name for *Dizygotheca elegantissima*. It has leathery black-green leaves with lighter veins that spread fingerlike into 9 segments with saw-toothed edges. You can buy thumb-pot seedlings for terrariums or an old one large enough to sit under. *D. veitchii* is similar, with coppery green leaves, reddish undersides and red veins.

Dracaena

These leafy members of the lily family are fascinating to collect and then to arrange in a display. Plain green *Dracaena fragrans* occasionally yields sprays of white, fragrant flowers. It adapts well to dim light indoors. The *D. fragrans* varieties 'Massangeana' and 'Victoriae' have broad showy leaves. Some of the *D. deremensis* varieties, such as 'Roehrs Gold' and 'Janet Craig', have striped leaves and make truly dramatic container plants. *D. sanderiana* has white margined green leaves on slender cane stems. *D. marginata*, little known until recently, is now one of the most common house trees. Its red edged thin leaves grow tuft fashion atop trunks that naturally zigzag and curve. Broad leafed *D. surculosa* (formerly known as *D. godseffiana*), with white and gold splotches, is a miniature in comparison to the others; it may form red berries. Three lookalike, growalike relatives are Hawaiian ti (*Cordyline terminalis*), *Dianella* and *Pleomele*.

Fatsia

Sometimes called aralia, *Fatsia japonica* is a handsome evergreen foliage plant with bold, palmately lobed leaves of shiny green, occasionally variegated with white. It is a common year-round outdoor plant in frost-free climates, and should stay indoors more in northern climates. The smaller-scale *Fatshedera* is the hybrid of *Fatsia* and *Hedera* (English ivy); it has the leaves of *Fatsia* and the ivy's growing patterns.

Ferns

This group of plants is one of the oldest known to man, many varieties having been found as fossils dating from prehistoric times. Throughout the ages, ferns have remained one of the most favorite of plants. Today many varieties are available for growing as container plants, either indoors or in shaded areas outdoors. Ferns look attractive in hanging baskets, and there are tiny forms available for terrariums and dish gardens.

The Boston fern (*Nephrolepis exaltata* 'Bostoniensis') is probably the most common and easiest to grow, but there are other varieties of it, such as the frivolous 'Fluffy Ruffles', that provide a change from the ordinary.

Holly ferns (species of *Cyrtomium*) have leathery, hollylike leaves. Various kinds of *Polystichum* and *Polypodium*, especially *P. aureum* and its varieties, are dramatic plants with magnificent fronds.

Rabbit's foot fern (*Davallia*) is so known because of its fuzzy, creeping rhizomes. Delicate, airy fronds grow from them, helping to make it an especially beautiful hanging plant.

Staghorn ferns (*Platycerium*) resemble antlers and are best displayed in a container hung on a wall, while tiny ferns like *Pteris* make excellent accents in miniature dish garden landscapes.

The bird's-nest fern (*Asplenium nidus*) has vivid green, wide, leaflike fronds, giving this plant a distinctive look when displayed with other ferns.

Dracaena

Polystichum tsus-simense and *Pteris cretica* with *Selaginella kraussiana* (spreading club moss). Below: *Platycerium* (staghorn fern).

Boston fern

Davallia

Adiantum (Maidenhair fern)

Cibotium (Hawaiian tree fern)

Ficus pumila (Creeping fig)

Ficus elastica (Indian rubber plant)

Fittonia

Delicate maidenhair ferns (*Adiantum*) have many small wedge shaped leaflets on thin, wiry, black stems. They require a lot of moisture.

The Hawaiian tree fern (*Cibotium*) grows long lacy fronds from a thick trunk to a height of 30 feet or more.

Fig Plants

The large, diverse ficus family not only includes the edible fig, but also tropical trees and a number of ornamentals perfect for container gardening.

Creeping fig. *Ficus pumila* has tiny heart shaped leaves. This fast-growing trailing plant cascades from hanging baskets and pots placed on shelves. It also thrives well in terrariums and as a climber on damp surfaces. It likes both moisture and shade. *F. sagittata* 'Variegata' is a colorful climber or trailer for humid locations.

Edible fig. The tree that produces edible figs is *Ficus carica*. Its varieties produce green, yellow or purple fruit. It is one of the easiest deciduous fruit trees to grow. Plant it in a large tub with ordinary garden soil, give it lots of sun and keep it moist during the growing season. In cold climates, this tree will need complete winter protection. Dwarf forms are available, making seasonal mobility easier.

Fiddleleaf fig. This fig plant, *Ficus lyrata*, often called *F. pandurata*, makes a striking container plant. It has durable but paper-thin leaves of deep green with a pleasing, fiddlelike shape. It grows from 5 to 10 feet high.

Indian rubber plant. *Ficus elastica* and the larger leaved *F. elastica* 'Decora' are old favorites. They have bold, deep green leaves on stems that reach from 2 to 10 feet tall. *F. elastica* 'Variegata' has colorful leaves that make a moiré of grassy green, metallic gray and creamy yellow.

Mistletoe fig. *Ficus deltoidea* is an interesting miniature upright tree. It grows up to about 36 inches tall, and produces many perfect little figs that have no food value. Its small rounded leaves are flecked with translucent silver. In bright sun the fruits turn red.

Weeping fig. *Ficus benjamina* has become very popular as a container plant. It is easy to see why this tree is selected for well-appointed spaces. The bark is birchlike and its graceful branches are loaded with glossy, willowlike leaves. Unfortunately, large specimens are often abused by placing them in the wrong environment as mere decoration. The plants are usually available from 2 to 15 feet high.

Give the weeping fig good light and evenly moist soil, with moderately high humidity. Be prepared for a period of adaptation to its new environment. Often the tree will lose most of its leaves when it is moved. Proper care will make it flourish again.

Fittonia

The beautiful white veined leaves shown at left belong to *Fittonia verschaffeltii* variety *argyroneura*. Another variety features pink veins, while the variety *pearcei* has intense red veins against olive green, paper-thin backgrounds. The plants grow semi-upright or trail gracefully over their containers. Small plants are good for terrariums.

Gynura

A sun-worshiping plant covered with brilliant purple hairs, *Gynura aurantiaca*, commonly called purple passion, is especially suited to hanging baskets. For its own survival, this plant should not be pampered. Occasionally it blooms tiny yellow flowers.

Ficus lyrata (Fiddleleaf fig)

Gynura

Ficus carica (Edible fig)

Mistletoe fig

Hypoestes

Iresine

Ivies: *Hedera helix* 'Curlilocks' and
Hedera canariensis 'Variegata', below.

Homalomena

This showy foliage plant is related to the *Philodendron*, and shares with it a love of tropical warmth and moisture. *Homalomena humilis* forms a rosette of plain green, pointed leaves; *H. wallisii* has dark olive green, reflexed, oval leaves, dramatically marked with areas of silver.

Hypoestes

This is a rapid-growing plant generously freckled with pink splotches on green, oval leaves (pink polkadot). The more sunlight it receives the more intense are its markings, making a cheerful addition to your collection. Spikes of lavender flowers may appear. A new variety with white polkadots has recently been introduced.

Iresine

The foliage of this plant has an intensely red color as evidenced by the photograph of an *Iresine* combined with baby's tears. Other varieties have yellow and green areas. Leaves are notched at the tips, giving it the name chicken gizzard. These small plants add brilliant accents to groupings.

Ivy

Many plants are called ivy, but the most famous is *Hedera helix* or English ivy. It is available in countless varieties. Some have typical English ivy leaves, except that they are smaller. 'Merion Beauty' is an example. 'Itsy Bitsy' is an example of a tiny variety. Others have the same leaves, except that they curl, wave or crinkle. 'Curlilocks' is an example. Some others have color variegations, like the yellow-gold and green of 'California Gold'.

Algerian ivy (*Hedera canariensis*) is also a superb foliage plant with large, bright green, leathery leaves.

All of these ivies are good climbers and will attach themselves by means of aerial roots to rough surfaces, such as a brick fireplace wall. They also make unsurpassed groundcovers for large planters. Even in poor light, a healthy plant of English ivy will decorate a coffee table for months. Ivies are excellent in hanging baskets and can be trained into interesting topiary shapes for whimsical touches in plant collections. They can be easily trained, espalier style, onto a container trellis. Trailing plants give a soft effect to groupings of container plants.

Joseph's Coat

This is the common name for *Alternanthera ficoidea*, a low foliage plant with small, round, corrugated leaves of red, yellow, cream, chartreuse and green. It is best used alone in a container. Pinching the tips helps Joseph's coat to grow low and bushy. The cultivar 'Bettzickiana' is a miniature version.

Liriope

Part of the fun of container gardening is making attractive arrangements of your plants. For an effective touch of graceful, grassy leaves, grow pots of the clump-forming *Liriope muscari* (plain green leaves, violet flowers in season) and the *L. muscari* 'Variegata' (cream striped leaves). The related *Ophiopogon* is equally easy to grow and showy.

Norfolk Island Pine

This evergreen tree with tiers of needle-set branches is *Araucaria heterophylla*. In time it grows large enough to decorate at Christmas. It needs winter warmth, but likes a summer vacation outdoors in a shady, moist spot. Seedlings are fine for dish gardens. Other araucarias, including the monkey puzzle (*A. araucana*), are less suited to container gardening.

Palms

These slow-growing plants have the ability to tolerate lack of light, drafts of cold, hot or dry air, and general neglect—and always provide accent, mood and interest.

Miniature palm seedlings of *Chamaedorea elegans* (often sold as *Neanthe bella*) are useful in terrariums.

The fish-tail palms are *Caryota mitis* and *C. urens*. *Chamaedorea erumpens* and *C. seifrizii* are the bamboo palms. *Chamaedorea elegans* is the popular parlor palm.

The butterfly or "areca" palm is *Chrysalidocarpus lutescens*. An old standby is the long-lasting kentia palm (*Howea*). Fan shaped palms are the bushy *Chamaerops*, *Licuala*, *Livistona* and *Rhapis* with bamboolike hairy canes. A graceful fernlike palm is *Phoenix roebelenii*, the dwarf date palm.

Pandanus

This plant is called the screw pine because the cornlike, prickly edged leaves spiral upward, corkscrew fashion, into a compact rosette. Some have vertical white stripes, while others have burgundy edges. Aerial roots grow downward, searching for moist soil. This tough but graceful plant looks charming potted in an urn and displayed on a pedestal. Its care is almost foolproof, and it remains pest free.

Pellionia

Pellionia provides a delightful foliage "fabric" with which to carpet the bare ground around large container plants. Or use it in terrariums, bottle gardens and baskets. *P. daveauana* has dark, brown-green leaves with a broad center area of metallic silver-green. *P. pulchra* has dark brown-green leaves heavily netted with silver-green veins.

Kentia palm *(Howea)*

Rhapis

Pandanus

Chamaedorea elegans

Liriope

Pellionia

Peperomias: *Peperomia caperata,*
P. griseoargentea and *P. obtusifolia.*

Philodendrons: *Philodendron* 'Emerald
Queen' and *P.* 'Orlando'.

Peperomia

These small plants grow mostly in compact rosettes with crinkled or plain heart shaped leaves. In season, spikes of tiny flowers make the plants look like visitors from outer space. The most common species is *Peperomia argyreia* (known to gardeners as *P. sandersii*), the watermelon begonia. It is neither a watermelon nor a begonia, but rather a member of the black pepper family. There are dozens of other peperomias; they are easy to grow, fun to collect. The leaves vary from black-green to glistening silver.

Philodendron

This plant's popularity is amazing. Since the early 1940s it has risen from near obscurity to become one of the most popular container plants. Beginning gardeners almost always have a *Philodendron* in their collection.

Ironically, the two plants most generally known as philodendrons are related, but are known botanically by other names. One of them, also called devil's ivy and pothos, is *Epipremnum* (see page 103); the other is *Monstera deliciosa,* known as *Philodendron pertusum* while it is a young plant.

Philodendron species divide themselves fairly neatly into two groups—those that climb and those that don't (called self-heading). Hybridizers have crossed the two groups, however, and now there are intermediate varieties. The climbers and semiclimbers need a moist totem pole to climb—they will do poorly without this means of support. Materials for the pole include pressed osmunda fiber (available at plant counters) and pieces of bark. Or you can make your own by wrapping a piece of ½-inch chicken wire around moist, unmilled sphagnum moss. The air roots of the *Philodendron* will attach themselves to the totem.

Perhaps no plant is sturdier than the *Philodendron,* which is able to grow under almost any condition. Most people are familiar with these common climbing plants, to the point of boredom. Yet this family offers a wealth of forms, color and foliage texture that should not be overlooked.

Philodendrons make good plants for hanging baskets; they can be trained on poles or used to fill a gigantic bare space, indoors or out. They will not tolerate freezing, however. The architectural quality of the larger self-heading varieties makes them of great interest to designers and decorators. The bold leaves offer an interesting contrast to smaller, more delicate plants.

Piggyback

The popular piggyback plant grows its leaves in an interesting fashion. The slightly hairy, heart shaped leaves of bright green grow from a basal rosette. At maturity each of the leaves sends up a new plantlet at the point where it joins its own stem, hence its common name. Since many of these new plants are produced on a single plant, it is also referred to as mother-of-thousands. These new plants may be cut off and rooted whenever they appear. *Tolmiea menziesii,* wilts whenever it needs water and rapidly returns to its original crispness when given sufficient water. Avoid severe drying out. (See page 126.)

Pilea

The popular silver splashed aluminum plant is *Pilea cadierei; P. microphylla* ejects pollen to rate the name artillery fern. Both have succulent stems that grow to 12 inches or more in length and the ability to withstand neglect. They are excellent for foliage contrast and accent in planter arrangements and good for individual pots, too. *P. involucrata,* sometimes called the panamiga, is also known as the South American friendship plant. *P. nummulariifolia* is often called creeping Charlie. The black leafed panamiga (*P. repens*) adds still another color to this family of durable foliage plants. A relative newcomer to the group is 'Moon Valley', which has bright chartreuse leaves and bronze markings.

Polyscias

A group of delicate-looking plants that are really quite sturdy, species of *Polyscias* are often called ming trees or aralias. They are available as tiny seedlings as well as huge specimens with marvelously gnarled trunks. *P. balfouriana* has rounded, dark green, leathery, spinachlike leaves; one of its varieties, 'Marginata', is edged in creamy white. *P. fruticosa* has clusters of fine, delicate leaves that look much like parsley. *P. filicifolia* is a bushy plant with bright green, fernlike foliage.

Pothos

Called devil's ivy or philodendron, pothos is correctly known botanically as *Epipremnum aureum*, although it has previously been called *Scindapsus aureus*. By any name it is a valuable plant. It grows in water for months, keeps in a planter for years or, given good, moist, humusy soil and filtered sunlight, will frame a window in record time. The pothos sold by florists has apple green, heart shaped leaves, boldly splashed with creamy white. Silver pothos ('Marble Queen') is creamier than it is green.

Prayer Plant

This is the common name for *Maranta leuconeura* variety *kerchoviana*. In the daytime it lays its bronze marked, satiny foliage flat; at night these leaves turn upward, like praying hands. It grows to about 8 inches tall. The variety *leuconeura* (previously known as *M. massangeana*) is even showier; it is sometimes called cathedral windows because the foliage colors remind one of stained glass. It looks beautiful in a terrarium or in a planter collection where other plants will help keep the air near it moist.

Rhoeo

Tiny white or blue flowers held in shellike bracts inspire the name Moses-in-the-cradle for *Rhoeo spathacea*. Children especially love the unusual flowers and their biblical association. Green, lance shaped leaves with iridescent purple undersides grow in upright rosette fashion. *R. spathacea* 'Vittata' adds ivory stripes to the leaves.

Saxifraga

The misleading names of strawberry geranium or strawberry begonia are associated with this attractive little plant. Actually, it is not related either to strawberries, geraniums or begonias. *Saxifraga stolonifera* grows in rosette fashion with dark green, scalloped, fuzzy leaves, and with whitish veins and purple splotches underneath. Delicate white flowers tower on thin stems. Baby plants form at ends of long, thin red runners. *S. stolonifera* 'Tricolor' (pictured

Polyscias guilfoylei 'Victoriae'

Pothos

Maranta (Prayer plant)

Rhoeo

Saxifraga stolonifera 'Tricolor'

Pileas, from left to right: *Pilea microphylla*, *P.* 'Silver Tree', *P. cadierei* and *P.* 'Moon Valley'.

Selaginella

Sansevieria cylindrica (Snake plant)

Spathiphyllum

on page 103) is dramatic because of its variegated leaves in shades of green, creamy white and rose-pink. These plants add interest to terrariums and bowl gardens or make unusual hanging baskets or shelf plants.

Schefflera

See *Brassaia*, page 93.

Selaginella

These mossy or fernlike plants love humidity and are used profusely in bowl gardens and terrariums. *Selaginella pallescens* (sweat plant) has delicate fernlike fronds in bright green. *S. kraussiana* (spreading club moss) is a trailing groundcover. *S. uncinata* (peacock fern) glows with a blue haze.

Snake Plant

Because of its transversely striped leaves, this is the common name for the neglected, overplanted and misused *Sansevieria trifasciata*. A less kind name is mother-in-law's tongue, which refers to the plant's tough, never-say-die nature and sharp, pointed leaves. *S. cylindrica* (shown) has round, pointed leaves. Give sansevierias half a chance and nice pots, and they will become the showy accents they should be, even producing fragrant blooms.

Soleirolia

Baby's tears is the common name of this tiny compact creeper (*Soleirolia soleirolii*, formerly known as *Helxine*). The plant grows densely and makes an excellent terrarium groundcover. It likes humidity and grows rapidly in moist greenhouses. Both gold and green varieties are shown encircling the red *Iresine* in the photograph on page 100.

Spathiphyllum

Too often overlooked, this sturdy plant has glossy green leaves with white "flowers," which are actually callalike spathes on slender stems. *Spathiphyllum* 'Clevelandii' is most popular. Similar but smaller varieties are *S.* 'Wallisii' and *S. floribundum*. *S. cannifolium* has a pale green spathe that slowly becomes white as it opens to reveal the long-lasting bloom. *Spathiphyllum*, or peace lily, usually blooms in the winter, but flowers can appear in any season. New varieties have fragrance, but lovely foliage and easy care are still their best features.

Two varieties of Swedish ivy

Swedish Ivy

Plectranthus australis is the waxy, leathery leaved, bright green, trailing member of the mint family, commonly known as Swedish ivy, although its is neither from Sweden nor an ivy. It produces spikes of white flowers, and makes a good-looking hanging basket plant. Variegated varieties, such as *P. oertendahlii*, *P. coleoides* and the cultivar 'Purpuratus', have shadings of silver, purple and gray-greens, and yield pink or lavender blossoms. *Plectranthus* are some of the most satisfactory basket plants—they grow fast, are easily trimmed and are highly tolerant of their environment.

Syngonium

This popular foliage plant is often confused with *Philodendron*—and it is closely related. *Nephthytis* is another name for *Syngonium*. The most common variety is sold as 'Tri-leaf Wonder'. Other, newer-named kinds that are more worthwhile, but just as easy to grow, are 'Imperial White', 'Green Gold' and 'Ruth Fraser'. In their juvenile stage, all form low mounds of arrowhead leaves. Later, they climb and need some kind of moss totem pole or rough bark on which to attach their aerial roots.

Wandering Jew

This common name covers several members of the spiderwort family, grown for their trailing, showy foliage. Leaves alternate along thick, succulent stems. Naturals for hanging baskets or as trailing plants on shelves or sills, these ornamentals are also attractive on pedestals or in pots for tables or window gardens. Sunlight intensifies their coloration, making them welcome additions to groupings of green foliage plants.

Tradescantias are small trailers with oval leaves, brightly variegated in shades of white, purple, blue-green, red, bright green, brown and gold. They are also called inch plants. Some varieties produce small flowers. Good trailing varieties include *Tradescantias albiflora* 'Albovittata', *T. albiflora* 'Laekenensis' ('Rainbow'), *T. blossfeldiana* and *T. navicularis* (chain plant).

Gibasis is the Tahitian bridal veil, so called because of its delicate, rambling stems and tiny white flowers. The small, dark green leaves have undersides of brownish purple.

Zebrina varieties have fleshy stems and pointed leaves that are vividly collored in lengthwise stripes of green, purple, silver, yellow, pink or red. Colors are intensified by sunlight. *Z. pendula* is purple with bands of silver. *Z. pendula* 'Quadricolor' sports bands of white with stripes of purple and pink.

Setcreasea is a purple leafed plant covered with white hairs. It produces tiny yellow or lavender flowers and the common name for it is purple heart. It does not trail like other members of the family, but retains a more erect, compact shape, making it a good tabletop plant.

Cyanotis is a small creeping plant, its leaves and stems covered with hair. *C. kewensis* is called the teddybear vine because of its brown hair. *C. somaliensis* is green with white hair and is called pussy ears. The most colorful is *C. veldthoutiana* (more correctly called *Tradescantia sillamontana*) with dark green leaves, reverses in purple, and purple stems. The plant is covered with thick, white, woollike hairs.

Variegated *Tradescantia*

Zebrina pendula

SHRUBS AS HOUSEPLANTS

Some shrubs can be grown as container plants all year long, indoors or outdoors according to your own climate.

Common or uncommon, shrubs take on new dimensions of beauty and usefulness when you grow them in movable containers.

The jet age is largely responsible for the recent ability to grow shrubs in containers. No matter how far north you live, you can grow pots or tubs of such tropical beauties as Chinese hibiscus, *Bougainvillea*, croton and *Allamanda*.

Probably all you have to do to obtain them is to visit your local nursery, for today exotic tropicals are routinely shipped all over the country by wholesale growers in Florida and California. These shrubs are meant to be grown in containers—which can be wheeled outdoors on a dolly during warm, frostfree weather, then moved back inside when the temperature turns cold.

If you are fortunate enough to live in a frostfree climate, you may already know how easy it is to rotate a selection of containerized flowering and foliage shrubs indoors and outdoors. When they are in peak bloom or berry, they can be used for display. When the show is over, they can go back to their more mundane growing space in the garden outside.

Not all container shrubs are cold-sensitive tropicals. You can grow any shrub or small tree—broad leafed or evergreen—in a tub or planter. Be sure the growing medium never dries out severely. Use lots of moisture-retentive peat moss in your mix, or use one of today's soilless mediums. Feed every 2 weeks.

Allamanda

Allamanda cathartica (golden trumpet) has large, shiny, yellow trumpet flowers that bloom profusely from April to September. It is a tropical vine and grows well in a tub or pot if given a supporting trellis. It can also be trained to form an arbor or pruned to the shape of a small tree or shrub. It needs sun, but may need some shade outdoors in the summer.

Ardisia

This bushy evergreen shrub is easily kept under 2 feet as a container plant. You can prune it into a bush, a little topiary tree, a bonsai or a plant for a hanging basket. Pinkish flowers in the spring are followed by crimson berries that last from fall to spring or longer. It is not frost hardy. Indoors, *Ardisia crenata*, or coral berry, does best in a cool, moist, sunny place.

Aucuba

This is the plant that you will often see for sale today on plant counters in supermarkets. It is an evergreen shrub that will tolerate outdoor climates down to about 15°F. It makes a very ornamental indoor plant. *Aucuba japonica* 'Variegata' or gold-dust plant is the kind to buy. Its leathery leaves have a high

Aucuba (Gold dust tree)

Ardisia

Bougainvillea

Coffea

Allamanda

Camellia

gloss with small blotches of butter yellow. Inconspicuous purple flowers on female plants are followed by scarlet berries if a male plant is nearby.

Azalea

The plants we call azaleas are actually members of the genus *Rhododendron* in the heath family. Most of the plants sold for container gardens are force-grown by florists in greenhouses. They are usually delicate varieties like *R. indica*. When one is brought home it should be kept constantly moist. Coolness prolongs the blooming season. Two years are usually required for complete recovery from the forcing. This can be accomplished by summering outdoors in a cool, partially shaded area. Bring it inside in the autumn; keep it cool and evenly moist. In January move it to a sunny, cool place, provide it with more water and feed it every 2 weeks.

Nursery raised azaleas thrive well as container plants, producing masses of blooms that can be white, yellow, orange, pink, red or scarlet. Select either sun-loving or shade-growing azaleas. In mild climates, they will grow all year long in containers outdoors. In more severe climates, put them outdoors in the summer and give them lots of light when they are indoors in the winter. Azaleas can be trained as standards, grown as bushes, or even placed in hanging baskets (shown on page 107). They make excellent subjects for a moist, airy, cool home greenhouse.

Bougainvillea

One of the showiest flowering shrubs is *Bougainvillea glabra*, an evergreen tropical vine from South America. It climbs vigorously, producing cascades of brilliantly colored bracts that last for a long time in various seasons. Colors of *Bougainvillea* hybrids include magenta, peach, rose, white, pink and orange. Pruned and shaped, it does well as a potted plant, but needs full sun and should not be left outdoors if night temperatures fall below 55°F. Grows well on a trellis in a tub. Try growing it indoors to frame a window or as a bonsai.

Camellia

This member of the tea family has glossy, evergreen, toothed leaves that remain attractive all year long. Many of the hundreds of varieties can be grown in containers and made into compact plants. Camellias are treasured for their beautiful, long-lasting blooms, which occur in the fall, winter and spring.

C. japonica ranges in color from white to dark red, with variegations of every combination in single or double blooms.

C. reticulata produces spring flowers of rose-purple. It is a good plant for greenhouse culture, as is *C. sasanqua*, which flowers in autumn and winter. Its fragrant white blooms are more delicate looking than those of other species. Other colors for both single and double flowers range from pink to dark rose, some of which are faintly scented.

C. saluenensis is a compact camellia, extremely hardy, with beautiful foliage. It produces an abundance of flowers in white, pink, rose and dark red.

Camellias can be maintained as shrubby potted plants and trained as standards. Or you may select special hanging basket types. In cold climates, camellias will survive where temperatures stay above 25°F.

Chenille Plant

The chenille plant (*Acalypha hispida*) is also called a red-hot cattail because of the long flowers it produces each summer. Originally from the East Indies, where it reaches a height of 15 feet, it seldom grows higher than 3 feet here. It does well indoors in a sunny, humid atmosphere, outdoors in warmth and partial shade.

Clerodendrum

Clerodendrum thomsoniae, called bleeding heart and glorybower, is a tropical plant that grows outdoors the year around in Southern California and Florida. For indoor-outdoor container culture, you will find it amenable to pruning and training as a shrub or on a trellis. Clusters of crimson flowers, each set in a white calyx, make a stunning display. *C. fragrans*, called Cashmere Bouquet, is a shrub that grows up to 8 feet high. It has the quality of Beauty and the Beast —clusters of white-pink flowers have a delightful fragrance, as its common name implies, while the leaves are foul smelling. *C. speciosisimum* has scarlet flowers.

Coccoloba

This is a common dune cover all over the tropics and is worth growing as an indoor-outdoor container plant. *C. uvifera*, the sea grape, has large green leaves, at first so red that they appear to be flowers. The actual flowers are white, followed by edible purple fruit. *C. diversifolia* is slightly smaller, with greenish white flowers and purple fruit.

Coffea

The plant that produces the coffee bean is an evergreen originating in Asia and tropical Africa. *C. arabica*, which produces beans of particularly high quality, is extremely adaptable to climate and is popular as a container plant. It has dark green leaves, fragrant white flowers and bright red berries. Coffee "beans" are the seeds inside the berries.

Croton

The croton is a showy tropical evergreen shrub with oblong leathery leaves that come in flamboyant colors and patterns, some wrinkled or curled. They exude a milky juice when injured, like many other members of the euphorbia family. Insignificant white flowers and tiny round fruits may appear. Most of today's varieties stem from the species *Codiaeum variegatum* variety *pictum*. Color is intensified by sunlight. If you can provide the proper cultural conditions, no foliage plant can rival the croton in attractiveness.

Elaeagnus

An evergreen shrub with durable, leathery leaves, *Elaeagnus pungens* can be grouped to contrast with plain foliage. Dark green leaves have undersides of silver and grow on brown, scale-covered branchlets. In the fall, clusters of silvery fragrant flowers appear, then small fruit covered with scales of brown and silver, which turn red as it ripens. Plants can be kept bushy and compact by pinching off the tips.

Chenille plant *(Acalypha)*

Clerodendrum

Croton

Elaeagnus

Euonymus

Flowering maple (Abutilon)

Fuchsia

Gardenia

E. pungens 'Maculata' adds yellow blotches to the leaves. *E. pungens* 'Tricolor' has variegation of pinkish white and yellow. The leaves of *E. pungens* 'Variegata' are pleasingly edged in yellowish white.

Euonymus

While this plant has become more popular for planting in outdoor gardens, some kinds are just as versatile for indoor pots and planters. Plants have small leaves of all green or variegations of yellow or white. Good upright varieties include *E. japonica* variety *albomarginatus*; *E. japonica* 'Variegatus'; *E. japonica* 'Yellow Queen', *E. japonica* 'Mediopicta'; and *E. japonica* 'Silver Queen'. If you want a neatly growing creeper, especially in a large planter, use *E. fortunei* 'Uncinata'. *Euonymus* makes a good bonsai plant or can be pruned to any desired shape.

Flowering Maple

This tropical shrub of the hollyhock family has maple shaped leaves. It blooms on new wood, like the related Chinese hibiscus, with pendant bells of white, yellow, pink, orange or red. It grows rapidly and best when planted in a large container. Indoors, give it sun; outdoors, dappled sun is fine. Prune to shape. *Abutilon megapotamicum* 'Variegata' makes a fantastic hanging basket plant.

Fuchsia

These are beautiful shrubs with simple green or variegated leaves and elegant pendant blooms. While the sepals enclosing most flowers are green, in fuchsias they are beautifully colored and flare open to reveal pendant petals of the same or another hue, often doubled. Stamens hang gracefully from the center of the petals. The color range goes from white to pink, red, lavender, violet, purple and blue, in countless combinations. Fuchsias bloom on new wood and should be pinched back to encourage bushy growth. They like a cool, moist climate. Provide a window sill or indoor gardening spot with nighttime coolness in the winter (68°F or less). Or grow fuchsias outdoors in a cool, shady place in the summer and buy new plants each spring.

F. hybrida includes popular specimens such as 'Carmelita' and 'Little Beauty'. The Magellan fuchsia (*F. magellanica*) is a densely branched plant. The trailing fuchsia (*F. procumbens*) is beautiful in hanging baskets.

Fuchsias can also be used as trailing shelf plants or upright bushy shrubs, or trained into standards.

Gardenia

If the heady aroma of these creamy, waxy looking blossoms pleases you, then try growing one in your container garden. The Cape jasmine (*G. jasminoides*) has large, glossy, dark green leaves and produces an abundance of flowers. Some varieties bloom in the summer, while others are winter bloomers. Gardenias kept indoors must have high humidity and cool nights (about 62°F), along with sunlight. They thrive in greenhouses.

G. jasminoides 'Floreplena' is a dwarf gardenia with small double flowers.

Gardenias can be maintained as shrublike bushes or, with patience, trained into standards. They require an acidic soil and can be successfully grown under artificial lights (see page 62).

Tabernaemontana divaricata, called the butterfly gardenia or crape jasmine, is a fragrant white-blooming shrub that is not a gardenia at all. Grow in a large tub and prune back in early spring to obtain many summer blooms.

Hibiscus

These flamboyant flowers are unequaled in splendor for indoor gardens where plenty of sunlight and warmth is available in winter. One species is

Hibiscus blossoms

known botanically as *Hibiscus rosa-sinensis*, commonly as Chinese hibiscus. Foliage is bright green or variegated, with coarsely toothed edges. Varieties come with single flowers the size of a dinner plate, in white and all shades of red, yellow, pink and salmon. There are kinds almost as big with double flowers. All are breathtakingly beautiful. Each flower lasts only one day, but healthy plants produce many buds. They grow on woody shrubs, and flower buds come onto the new wood so that the plants can be pruned to compact, small proportions for container use.

Ixora

This exotic hedge plant seen in gardens in the deep South is useful for pots and planters. It may be pruned and cut back severely without harm when well grown. Leaves are leathery and glossy green. Clusters of flowers, in abundance at almost any season, may be brilliant hues of scarlet, orange or rose, or the palest shades of pink, yellow or white. *I. coccinea* (shown here) is known as flame-of-the-woods. *I. javanica* has long slender leaves and red branches that yield huge clusters of showy waxlike flowers. They love sunlight and humidity and are excellent greenhouse plants.

Ixora coccinea

Lantana

A perennial sprawling shrub in mild climates, *Lantana* can be used as a container shrub or a hanging basket plant. The plants are easily pruned to keep whatever shape is desired and judicious pruning is one way to keep the plants flowering year around. Lantanas will do well in a sandy soil kept somewhat on the dry side, but for the best bloom they need lots of light. As the plants get older keep the heavier wood pruned out to maintain a healthy plant with full foliage. Popular for summer bedding in the colder parts of the country, lantanas can be lifted in the fall for winter bloom indoors. This is a good time to consider pruning again. After potting, place lantanas in the brightest window possible for best results. In milder areas they need no special care. Don't fertilize too often as this will result in more leaves and less flowers. Nurseries commonly offer two species: *L. camara* and *L. montevidensis*. *L. camara*, the shrubbier of the two, has flowers in varying tones of yellow, orange, and red, while the more sprawling *L. montevidensis* has lavender flowers.

Lantana

Mandevilla

This evergreen vine from Brazil is a showy container plant. You can expect it to climb to a height of 8 feet or more. Trellis training and a few well-placed snips with your pruning shears will keep it tidy. *M. splendens* has clusters of rosy pink flowers, each as much as 3 inches across. Leaves are long, leathery and dark green. The shrub is often sold as *Dipladenia*. Lesser known is *M. boliviensis*, which has white flowers that bloom all summer, into the autumn. In cold weather, keep cool but frost free, water less and withhold fertilizer.

Myrtle

Nandina

Oleander

Pittosporum

Privet

A new, smaller-growing, pink flowered *Mandevilla* is on the market now; it is especially good for container gardening (see page 12).

Myrtle

This evergreen herb is outstanding in indoor pots and planters. *Myrtus communis* has plain, glossy, dark green leaves. *M. Communis* 'Microphylla' is a smaller version. *M. communis* 'Variegata' combines green and creamy colors in its leaves. Myrtle foliage has a spicy odor when bruised, fragrant flowers, black berries. It is a perfect subject for topiary pruning.

Nandina

Nandina is an airy evergreen shrub from the Orient. *N. domestica*, known as heavenly bamboo, has narrow leaflets growing on canelike stems of green combined with pink-bronze, which turn dark red in the fall. Clusters of small white flowers bloom in the summer months, followed by shiny red berries. The plant thrives in moist container gardens.

Oleander

This old-fashioned plant with willowy stems and leaves is enjoying new popularity. It is good for large pots and tubs and has definite value for interior decoration. Hybrids have more spectacular blooms than the old kinds; try 'Comte Berthelemy' with double red flowers, and 'Mrs. Roeding' with double salmon-pink blooms. *Nerium oleander* 'Variegatum' has large gray-green leaves that are attractively edged with white, and red blossoms. The juice of the oleander is *poisonous*; do not burn pruned-off parts.

Pittosporum

This hardy evergreen shrub has great value for potting and planter use. Grown primarily for its shining green, leathery leaves in whorls, *Pittosporum tobira* also produces small, fragrant white flowers in clusters. *P. tobira* 'Variegata' leaves have white edges. This plant is excellent for large topiary training or bonsai work.

Podocarpus

A relative of the hardy evergreen yews that grow in gardens everywhere, this is almost without peer for use in planters and pots. *Podocarpus macrophyllus* has slender leaves and withstands severe trimming. You can maintain it as a compact bush or clip it to an unusual shape as a topiary subject. *P. nagi* has coarser leaves and spreading branches.

Privet

The wax-leaf privet (*Ligustrum lucidum*) is outstanding for pots and planters. It is characterized by very shiny leaves and clusters of creamy flowers that bloom in the summer. *L. obtusifolium* also produces a large crop of blackberries in the winter. The entire plant is *poisonous* if ingested. Privets will tolerate frequent trimming and therefore are easily trained to special shapes including topiary work and bonsai.

Pyracantha

Known as the firethorn, this thorny evergreen is now being widely used as a container plant. *Pyracantha coccinea* and its hybrids adapt well to bonsai dwarfing or to espaliering on a trellis set in a container. From May until June, white blossoms are followed in the autumn by scarlet, orange or yellow fruit that lasts into the winter, unless eaten by birds. Some pyracanthas remain hardy when temperatures drop as low as -10°F. Indoors in the winter they require a cool environment.

Rhododendron

Although the species we know as azaleas have always been cultivated to some extent in pots and other containers, it is much less common to grow other rhododendrons in this mobile way. One reason for growing them in containers is that in regions that have alkaline soil, it is easier to keep the soil acidic when it is confined to a tub or planter. Another reason is that in severely cold climates, some truly exotic but not terribly cold-hardy rhododendrons can be container grown—brought outdoors in the summer and kept indoors in the winter. They make superb plants for a cool greenhouse. The most exciting way to make your selection is to visit a nursery at flowering time and choose precisely the colors you want. Use an abundance of acidic peat moss in the container. Keep evenly moist at all times and place in dappled shade. Feed with an acid-type fertilizer.

Silk Oak

This elegant tree (*Grevillea robusta*) grows to 150 feet high in Australia, but if you start from seeds or buy a young plant, it makes a perfect indoor or potted patio tree. Ferny, frondlike leaves unfurl from downy silver shoots. It grows quickly and easily, indoors or outdoors, in semishade. In cold climates, be sure to bring the silk oak inside before the frost.

Stephanotis

This evergreen, twining vine (botanically known as *Stephanotis floribunda*) yields clusters of exquisitely formed, waxy, white, fragrant flowers that are a must for bridal bouquets. You can grow it as a fine container plant by training the vine onto a trellis and nipping it occasionally with your pruning shears or fingers. Give it sun indoors, a little shade outside. Keep moist but protect it from frost.

Sweet Olive

Most people who have visited New Orleans will recall the intoxicating, elusive fragrance given off by the tiny, everblooming white flowers of *Osmanthus fragrans*, which grows abundantly there. No better shrub can be found for potting. Indoors, keep it moist, cool and in the sun.

Tibouchina

This shrub tends to appear gawky, but it is worth growing for the showy purple flowers and elegant foliage. Some of the best specimens, in the ground or in containers, have been trained as standards (small trees). Pinch back young growth frequently to induce branching. In cold climates, keep indoors in a sunny, cool, moist place. This plant is not for a warm city apartment. *T. urvilleana*, also known as *T. semidecandra*, or princess flower, is the most popular. It responds to *Fuchsia* culture, and languishes in a hot, dry environment.

Rhododendron

Podocarpus   Silk oak

Stephanotis

Pyracantha

Tibouchina

Sweet olive

The sculptural quality of cactus and other succulents makes them a dramatic addition to the indoor landscape.

CACTI AND OTHER SUCCULENTS

The world of cactus and succulents is a huge, diverse and fascinating one. For the most part, the plants are well-suited for indoor container gardening, making them perfect for the collector.

There are enough cacti and other succulents to keep you fascinated for a lifetime! Succulents have the ability to store moisture inside their fleshy stems and leaves. They come both from desert and rain forest, and not all are thorny and leafless. The lemon vine or *Pereskia*, for example, has citruslike leaves and wicked thorns, plus showy, fragrant flowers—and it climbs. The *Opuntia* cactus bears edible prickly pears.

As container plants, virtually all cacti and other succulents have the ability to exist, if not thrive, in the normally dry, warm atmosphere of the average house. Some do need *partial shade*, certainly protection, from the full, burning sun during hot weather. Generally speaking, they appreciate a little dryness between waterings, but remember, a container of soil can become deathly dry even for these water-storing plants. A general rule is to water thoroughly, then allow the soil to become dry, and remain dry, for a couple of days before rewatering.

Try growing some of these vastly differing plants that qualify as succulents—some of them are very strange indeed.

Cacti

Serious collectors spend years searching out odd and unusual cacti. They have been so successful, in fact, that it is a bewildering decision to choose only a few plants. The best way is to visit specialists (or study their catalogs) and select those you find most appealing. Some choices are illustrated here. Prominent names include *Aporocactus, Astrophytum, Chamaecereus, Notocactus, Echinocereus, Opuntia, Echinopsis, Gymnocalycium, Rebutia, Lobivia* and *Mammillaria.*

Indoors, these all need as much direct sun as you can give them. Outdoors, they can take sun all day or as little as half a day. To maintain cacti indoors in a dimly lit place, spotlight them with incandescent floodlights placed 4 feet away and burned 14 hours daily.

Succulents

Some succulents are one of a kind, while others represent whole families. All thrive on potted culture, indoors and outdoors; all need frost-free winter quarters. These succulents are commonly available: *Adromischus, Aeonium,* (some look like bronze red and green roses), *Aptenia* (an easy hanging-basket plant), *Beaucarnea* (or ponytail, an outstanding houseplant), *Cotyledon, Faucaria* (tiger's jaws), *Gasteria, Kleinia, Pedilanthus* and *Senecio rowleyanus* (string of pearls).

Aloe. These are easily cultivated succulent members of the lily family. Some, like *Aloe aristata,* remain as ground-hugging rosettes for so long that they can be considered miniatures. Others, like the *Aloe vera* (actually *A. barbadensis*), grow leaves up to 24 inches long. Small kinds for pots and planters are *A. variegata, A. humilis* and *A. brevifolia.* Larger kinds are *A. barbadensis, A. ciliaris, A. striata* and *A. arborescens.*

Shade-tolerant succulents: **A.** *Hoya bella,*
B. *Pedilanthus tithymaloides,* **C.** *Senecio rowelayanus,* **D.** *Euphorbia tirucalli,*
E. *Hylocereus,* **F.** *Ledebouria socialis,*
G. *Hoya carnosa,* **H.** *Rhipsalis baccifera*
and **I.** *Synadenium grantii* 'Rubra'.

Agave. The true century plant, *Agave americana,* is too large for most container gardens, except while it is young. Better for long-term pot growing are the *A. americana* cultivars 'Medio-picta' and 'Marginata', as well as *A. miradorensis, A. pumila* and *A. victoriae-reginae.* These dramatic rosette plants make attractive accents when placed on patios, terraces, steps or balconies (see page 119).

Crassula. There are hundreds of kinds of *Crassula,* treasured for their shape, color and growth habits. Most will bloom in season when given warmth and sunlight. Indoors and outdoors; in pots, baskets and dish-garden desertscapes; and under fluorescent lights, crassulas grow easily and well (see page 119).

Cycas. Plants in the family Cycadaceae generally fall into the slow and easy-to-grow class. Most make ideal houseplants and attractive bonsai specimens. Because they are so slow growing they can be kept in the same pot for many years, in effect becoming an "heirloom plant" capable of being handed down from one generation to the next. In nature they often grow in rocky areas, so being pot bound is almost a natural condition, which the cycads don't seem to mind. *Cycas revoluta,* commonly referred to as the sago palm, is a popular variety. These palmlike plants have thick succulent trunks. Many stiff, narrow green leaflets are borne on arching green stems in a whorled arrangement. Members of the closely related genera *Ceratozamia, Dioon, Enchephalartos,* and *Zamia* share cycas' leaf arrangement though foliage color, texture, and shape varies from group to group.

Cycads bear cones at the top of their trunks (when mature). The female plants have larger cones, and plants of both sexes must bear cones simultaneously to produce viable seed.

Echeveria. As a rule, these hen-and-chickens succulents make geometrically perfect rosettes of leaves close to the ground; some look like glorious green roses. Grow them in pots or pottery strawberry jars; for large hangings, try moss-stuffed wire balls. Recommended are *Echeveria crenulata, E. derenbergii, E. elegans, E. multicaulis* and *E. pulvinata* (see page 118).

Euphorbia. These succulent relatives of the Christmas poinsettia (*Euphorbia pulcherrima*) are weird and wonderful. The most popular *Euphorbia* is the crown-of-thorns (*E. milii*). For a bold accent, try the cow's horn (*E. grandicornis*), hat rack *(E. lactea)* or pencil cactus *(E. tirucalli).* For pure fascination, try Medusa's head *(E. caput-medusae), E. bupleurifolia* and closely related *Synadenium,* or red milk bush (see above and page 119).

Kalanchoe. These succulents are closely related to *Echeveria*; both are in the crassula family. Some are grown primarily for their interesting foliage: *Kalanchoe tomentosa, K. marmorata, K. tubiflora, K. pinnata* (baby plants form in the air on old leaves) and treelike *K. beharensis.* Others, especially *K. blossfeldiana* (and its named cultivars like 'Tom Thumb', 'Vulcan' and 'Brilliant Star'), *K. flammea* and *K. uniflora,* are cultivated for their cherry, orange-red, apricot or yellow flowers, which appear after the buds have been initiated by the shortest days of the year (see pages 118 and 119).

Mistletoe cactus. These cacti of the genus *Rhipsalis,* are strange in appearance, and look almost like true mistletoe. They do well in baskets, pots and planter boxes. Grown for their bright green foliage, in season the blooms are an added treat. They thrive in a moist atmosphere with some shade, very much like bromeliads. *Hatiora* (drunkard's dream) is related, and is also fun to grow.

Above: **A.** *Echeveria elegans.* **B.** *Lithops bella* (living stones) and **C.** *Beaucarnea recurvata* (ponytail palm).

Orchid cactus. These beautiful flowers are as lovely as orchids, but are shaped more like water lilies. Foliage is not cactuslike, but leafy; they are sometimes planted in hanging baskets and placed in semishade. *Epiphyllum* is the scientific name and the most common species, *E. oxypetalum*, is one of the easiest of the night-blooming species to grow. Specialists can recommend small-growing hybrids that are best suited to growing indoors in freezing weather.

Sedum. Hundreds of *Sedum* species grow well in containers. Favorites include *S. pachyphyllum* (jelly bean), *S. treleasei, S. rubrotinctum, S. stahlii, S. dasyphyllum* (miniature creeper) and *S. multiceps* (little Joshua tree). An outstanding hanging-basket plant is *S. morganianum*; shield it from wind and broiling sun and give it a moist atmosphere.

Stapelia. These succulents are sometimes called carrion-fly plants because their flowers have an odor that tricks flies into thinking a dead animal is about. But stapeliads have such fantastic, star shaped flowers that many people tolerate them, odor and all. They need summer shade and winter sun. *S. gigantea* has star flowers up to 12 inches in diameter. *S. hirsuta* has 4-inch furry star flowers. *S. variegata* has 2-inch stars and a less noticeable odor than the others.

Stone plant. These incredible little succulent bodies seem to belong to the mineral kingdom. Collect species of *Lithops, Dinteranthus, Pleiospilos* and *Conophytum*, and have fun searching for lookalike stones to place in pots with them. Stone plants can be grown indoors or outdoors, as well as in fluorescent lit gardens. Some have daisylike flowers.

Wax plant. The leaves and fragrant flowers of *Hoya* are thick and waxy. This plant does well in a hanging basket and as a vine. Cuttings grow easily for long periods in water. The choicest specimens are the variegated forms of *H. carnosa* and the miniature *H. bella* (see page 116).

Windowed succulents. These wonders of nature, related to stone plants, have translucent "window" areas in the top of each fat, clublike stem. One popular kind is *Fenestraria aurantiaca*, which grows less than 2 inches tall. Some common haworthias, such as *Haworthia cymbiformis*, also have translucent leaf tips. Nature uses the windows to admit light to sand covered plants.

A. Ruffled *Echeveria crenulata,*
B. *Kalanchoe beharensis,* **C.** *Sempervivum tectorum* in owl planter, **D.** Golden barrel (*Echinocactus grusonii*) and
E. *Ferocactus acanthodes.*

A. *Euphorbia inermis,* **B.** *Agave expansa,* **C.** *Crassula* (African species), **D.** *Kalanchoe tomentosa* (Panda bear plant), **E.** *Agave filifera,* **F.** blooming *Rubutia* collection, **G.** *Sedum* (a ground cover), **H.** collection of euphorbia, **I.** *Crassula falcata,* **J.** hanging basket of *Portulacaria afra* 'Variegata', **K.** the giant specimen *Pachycereus pringlei* and **L.** *Espostoa lanata.*

PROPAGATING

Plant multiplication or propagation that you do at home is one way to have lots of container plants— as unusual as you like—for very little money. And few aspects of gardening, or of any hobby for that matter, are as rewarding.

Almost all seed catalogs offer the seeds of common houseplants. You will find *Begonia semperflorens*, geranium hybrids, gloxinia, *Cyclamen*, *Kalanchoe* and calla lily. In more comprehensive listings you will find ferns, *Schefflera* (*Brassaia*), *Fuchsia*, and *Jatropha*. Search out the silk oak, or *Grevillea*, which grows easily from seeds, first forming a fernlike bush, but rather quickly growing into a small tree just right for a bright spot indoors or as a patio specimen. Other houseplants to start from seed are: African violets, bromeliads, cacti, *Calceolaria*, cineraria, crape myrtle and *Peperomia*.

Actually, the list of seeds available is practically endless. The most unusual seeds are often available through membership in one of the houseplant societies, for example the American Begonia Society or the American Gloxinia and Gesneriad Society; for addresses, see page 140. But even for the common varieties, planting from seed is a money-saving method. Seeds cost only pennies compared to the purchase of plant seedlings.

Certainly not to be overlooked are pits and seeds from the kitchen. You can grow fine foliage plants from avocado pits, citrus seeds or sprouted sweet and Irish potatoes and onions. Health food stores offer all kinds of seeds that you can have fun sprouting. A handful of bean or pea seeds planted thickly on the surface of moist soil, either in a pot or shallow tray, will quickly repay you with a lush patch of greenery. Actually, any seed is fair game for sprouting indoors, and it may just turn into a unique container plant!

Planting Seeds

A seed is merely a container for a dormant tiny plant waiting for the right conditions to continue the life cycle. To achieve this it must be given a disease-free growing medium, proper warmth and moisture and adequate light for germination.

Many gardeners today find vermiculite or milled sphagnum moss successful starting mediums because of the ease in lifting out the seedlings without damaging the roots. A mixture of peat moss and vermiculite also makes a good growing medium. By using soilless mixes, you can avoid losing many seedlings due to damping off—a weakening of the stems at soil level caused by disease organisms in garden soil and composts or standing water. If you decide to use compost or garden soil or to add either to a soilless mix, you should sterilize it first. You can sterilize soil by putting it in the oven for about 2 hours at 160 to 180°F.

Use medium-size flats, cartons, pots or any container you desire. Cottage cheese containers with transparent or translucent snap-on lids are perfect for starting many seeds. With the lid in place you have a self-contained growth chamber which will not need further watering until the seedlings have grown to a reasonable size and are ready for transplanting. Placed in subdued light at an appropriate termperature, germination will be surprisingly rapid in this in-

Once the seedlings are up, the next step is to plant them in small, individual containers. Plants from seed cost only a fraction of those purchased when fully grown.

expensive, ideal environment. Check the recommended depth for the particular seed on the seed packet. If in doubt about how deep to plant, remember this general rule: Cover each seed to the depth of its own thickness. Scatter tiny dustlike seeds on top of moist growing medium. But remember to sow seeds sparingly. Seedlings that are bunched together do not receive the proper circulation of air and it makes transplanting a chore, also.

Firm the area around the seed by pressing down gently. Label each starter container with the name of the plant, the date planted and any other desired information. Water lightly, then slip the seed container into a plastic bag or cover it with paper. Check seed packets to see whether specific light is required for germination. Follow directions. Bottom heat (70 to 75°F) may be added to expedite germination. Inexpensive soil heating cables are available in sizes to meet your needs. Your gardening center can secure the best type of unit for your use.

Growing Seedlings in Blocks, Cubes and Pellets

Seeds may be sown directly into any of the small, compacted, synthetic soil units on the market (Jiffy 7 Pellets, BR8 Blocks, Kys-Kubes) after they have been throroughly moistened. Place them in a warm spot for germination. Cover them with paper or place them in plastic bags to prevent drying out. Once moistened, they will contain all the water necessary for sprouting. After the little seedlings have appeared, remove covers.

Caring for Seedlings

Check seeds daily, adding water if necessary. When seedlings begin to show, move containers into brighter light. The first two leaves to sprout (cotyledons) nourish the stem tip and the foliage leaves that follow. Wait for foliage leaves to appear before placing seedlings in sunshine. A rule of thumb is to give seedlings the same amount of light as you would to the mature plant. Twelve hours a day is generally recommended for foliage plants and five hours for flowering ones. If sunlight is impossible to find, seedlings will do just as well placed 6 inches below two 40-watt fluorescent tubes, burned 16 hours out of every 24. Adjust the height of the lamps as necessary during growth.

When seedlings begin active growth, fertilize every other week with a diluted liquid solution—1/3 to 1/2 of the regular strength.

Seed Starting Containers

Here are some of many available in your area.

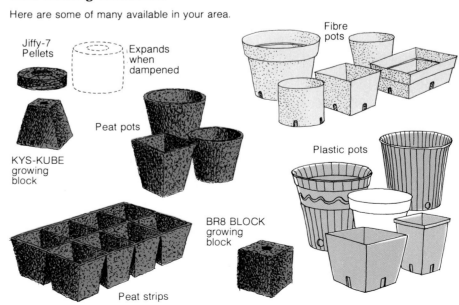

Jiffy-7 Pellets — Expands when dampened

KYS-KUBE growing block

Peat pots

Peat strips

BR8 BLOCK growing block

Fibre pots

Plastic pots

Two step method

STEP 1

Sow seeds in a small tray of vermiculite. Be sure medium is thoroughly damp before seeding. Set seeds about ¼ inch deep and about 2 inches apart. Cover seeds and water lightly. Slip tray into plastic bag and keep at about 75°. No water is necessary until after germination and then only enough to keep vermiculite damp, not soaked.

STEP 2

When the first true leaf is formed the seedlings are ready to go into 3″ to 4″ peat or plastic pots filled with soil mix (see text).

Pull seedling from vermiculite and set in small hole in soil mix so seed leaves (cotyledons) are about ½ inch from soil.

Press soil firmly around roots and stem.

Put pots on a tray and in a plastic bag until ready for hardening off. Wickets of coat hanger wire will keep plastic above plants.

One step method

Sow seeds, 2 at a time, directly into plastic pots, peat pots, Kys-cubes, RB8 blocks, Jiffy-7 pellets. Water thoroughly and place on a tray in a plastic bag. They'll be ready to transplant when about 6 inches high.

Transplanting Seedlings

As seedlings grow they must be given room for their roots to develop. It is time to transplant when they begin to crowd together. Start them off in individual 2¼-inch pots. Move them into larger containers one pot size at a time. The transition to large permanent pots should be done gradually as the plants mature.

Be creative when it comes to selecting containers for your young plants. For starters try: strawberry jars, sawed-off barrels, tubs, bushel baskets, hanging baskets. The possibilities are limitless; and don't forget the classic clay pot.

Make sure the first true leaves have formed before you transplant. Fill the container you have selected with soil—preferably a synthetic kind. Make a small hole in the container and set the seedling in it so that the leaves are ½ inch from the surface. Firmly press down the soil around the roots and stem. Water carefully.

If you are planning to put your new plants outside, make the transition gradually from the indoor environment. Begin by taking them out for a day, gradually giving them more sunlight and returning them to the indoors at night, particularly if any danger of frost is likely. Begin to expose them to lower temperatures about 2 weeks before setting them out permanently. And, of course, you may want to keep outdoor container plants indoors some of the time, too.

Now, sit back and watch your little plants grow. It will amaze you to watch them mature into productivity as you remember those first little leaves peeping up late last winter.

How to Root Cuttings

What great grandmother called slips we now call cuttings. To make a cutting, all you do is break or cut off a healthy piece of growth, usually 4 to 6 inches long —but this varies with the kind of plant. Strip or cut off all leaves from the lower half of the cutting. Then, using your index finger or a pencil, make a hole in the rooting medium, insert the bare-stem portion of the cutting, and firm it into place. Water well, encase the entire cutting and container in a plastic bag and set it in a shady, warm place.

You can tell when the roots have begun to grow because the foliage will perk up and the new plant will show signs of growing. At this stage you can remove the plastic cover for an hour or two daily, then you can leave it off for several hours, and finally you can discard the cover and move the plant to a good growing area—sun if it is a sun lover, shade if it is a shade plant. Transplant when the original pot is filled with roots.

Rooting Mediums. Different gardeners use different rooting mediums for cuttings. The most convenient one is water—just a drinking glass of tap water. This old-fashioned method fell out of favor a few years ago, but it seems to be making a comeback. Water rooted cuttings transplant easily into soilless mixes (see page 26). When you pot a cutting that has been rooted in water, just be sure that it is moistened very well, and then cover it with plastic for a few days.

Cuttings also root well when planted directly into a soilless mix. Or you can use straight vermiculite, perlite, milled sphagnum moss or a mixture of these with peat moss.

If you want to root a number of different cuttings, a clear plastic box makes an excellent propagator. Heat an ice pick to punch a few ventilation holes in the

Take a cutting from a geranium with a sharp knife. Remove lower leaves and any excessive top growth. Use a pencil to make a hole in moistened soilless medium. Then place the trimmed cutting in the pot. Cover for a few days with a plastic cup.

top. Add 2 inches of rooting medium in the bottom, moisten, then insert your cuttings. Put the lid on and set the box in a bright, warm place, but not in direct sun. You can make a similar propagating box by using a seed flat or fruit lug to hold the cuttings and a sheet of polyethylene plastic held up by wire coat hangers to create the "greenhouse" cover.

Rooting hormones. If you have read your seed catalogs closely or if you have read the labels while wandering down gardening center aisles, you may have noticed small containers of rooting hormones. These are excellent products. They promote faster rooting and better root systems. You don't really need a rooting hormone for such plants as coleus and Swedish ivy, which root almost overnight. But for other plants, especially anything bordering on being woody —*Fuchsia* and heliotrope, for example—rooting hormones are recommended.

Self-propagation

Some plants have the amazing ability to propagate themselves from a single leaf cutting. Best known for this are African violets, but the same technique works for rex and some other rhizomatous begonias, gloxinias, sedums, kalanchoes, even some philodendrons (trailers or climbers) and peperomias. Take leaf cuttings from a poinsettia for example, and allow them to dry or callous for a few hours by simply placing them on a surface that is out of the direct sun. When the cut surface—the base of the cutting—is dry, proceed with planting.

Tropical foliage plants that form a thick, trunklike stem, can be propagated from 4-inch cuttings. Remove any leaves and simply lay the "logs" on the surface of a moist rooting medium in a propagating box. Roots and new leaf growth will sprout from dormant eyes or leaf buds along the stem. This method works for Chinese evergreen (*Aglaonema*), *Alocasia, Dieffenbachia, Dracaena,* certain *Philodendron* species and *Pleomele*. These same plants can also be propagated by the method of air-layering.

Rooting trees and shrubs

Trees and shrubs can be propagated from softwood or hardwood cuttings. Softwood describes a year's growth, taken early or at midseason. Hardwood describes growth at the end of a season.

Softwood cuttings to try include *Abutilon, Acacia, Aralia,* Norforlk Island pine, *Ardisia,* blueberry, *Gardenia* and rose. *Ligustrum, Pyracantha, Forsythia, Weigela* and sweet olive can also be rooted. Hardwood cuttings include azalea, *Rhododendron,* boxwood, conifers and needle evergreens, grapes, dogwood and flowering trees.

Softwood cuttings. Prepare for planting softwood cuttings the same as you would for such houseplants as geraniums or angel-wing begonias. Cuttings do best in a cool, moist, airy, bright atmosphere; they should not have direct sun until the roots have formed. Some growers rig up a misting system with jets timed to mist the cuttings every few minutes.

Hardwood cuttings. Cuttings from hardwood are usually made in the autumn, sometimes after the frost has defoliated the deciduous types of trees and shrubs. Dip the base of each cutting into rooting hormone, then plant. Cover with plastic or glass and keep in moderate coolness (60 to 70°F). A cool fluorescent lit area, perhaps in the basement, makes an ideal environment in which to root hardwood cuttings. Cold-hardy types, such as evergreens, can be planted in a coldframe.

Seeds. Trees and shrubs can be started from seed, also. Winter-hardy kinds usually need to be subjected to freezing temperatures, followed by warmth, in order to break their dormancy. If you don't have a coldframe in which to do your planting, you can simulate winter in your freezer! Mix the seeds with moist sand and peat moss in a jar or plastic container. Freeze for 2 to 4 months, then plant in a warm, bright place.

Air layering is useful for salvaging leggy plants that look straggly and cannot grow lower leaves. Cut into the stem and insert a wedge, such as the prong of a plastic fork, to pry the stem open. Wrap in a plastic bag filled with damp sphagnum moss. Watch for roots to appear at the incision. Then cut the stem off just below the new roots. Pot the rooted plant in its own container and enjoy a compact plant.

Seeds are available of fine azalea hybrids—the Kaempferi, Exbury, Mollis and Kurume hybrids, for example. These tiny seeds require the same treatment that you would give gloxinias or begonias. Kept between 60 and 70°F, they will sprout in about 3 weeks.

Multiplying by Division

When multiple stems emerge from the base of a plant, you can divide them. Wax begonias, as well as most bromeliads, make good examples. Cluster-forming succulents, such as certain sedums and crassulas, and African violets that have not had their suckers removed have multiple stems. Sansevierias also multiply in this way—one healthy division sometimes fills a pot with other plants in a year's time.

The easiest way to propagate by division is to slice down through the soil with a sharp knife, severing a new plant from the old. It is helpful if you are able to gather some roots along with the newly cut off plant. But the main thing to remember is that you must get some of the main stem system; otherwise, the new plant cannot live.

The other way to divide is to knock the entire plant out of its pot. Then, with your hands gently pull away the soil until you fully expose the root system and framework of the plant. Cut or break apart the divisions and replant each one.

Division is an excellent way to multiply your supply of amaryllis, some *Haemanthus*, *Zephyranthes*, climbing onion (*Bowiea volubilis*), *Tulbaghia* and *Clivia*. The pregnant onion (*Ornithogalum caudatum*) forms pealike bulbils on the surface of the old bulb; all you have to do is pick them and plant them.

Tuber division. Dividing tubers is closely related to dividing plants with multiple basal stems or leaf rosettes. This division is possible for large bulbs of gloxinia, *Gloxinera*, tuberous begonia and *Caladium*. Simply cut apart the tuber like a potato, being sure that every part contains a bud or "eye." Dust the cut surface with a fungicide, then plant in moist rooting medium.

Stolon Propagation

Several common houseplants grow stolons or runners, strawberry fashion. These include the strawberry begonia (*Saxifraga stolonifera*), the flame violet (*Episcia*), some species of African violet, the spider plant (*Chlorophytum*) and the walking iris (*Neomarica*). One way to root them is to fill a small pot with moist rooting medium, place it alongside the mother plant and hairpin or tape the base of the stolon into the smaller pot. When active new growth signals that the baby has its own root system, you can sever it from the mother. The other way to propagate with stolons is simply to clip them off and insert the base of each in moist propagating medium, either in a community box or in individual pots. Cover with glass or with plastic film until the roots have formed.

The piggyback plant (*Tolmiea menziesii*) forms new plantlets on top of old leaves; these can be rooted in the same fashion as stolons.

Plantlets formed on stolons of the spider plant, above, and the piggyback plant, right, can be pinned into moist soil in separate pots. Keep pots alongside the mother plant until plantlets root, or separate them right away.

Starting Your Outdoor Garden Indoors

Flowers	Sowing Depth	Soil Temperature For Germination	Starting Time* (weeks before last killing frost)	Growing Tips
African daisy (Dimorphotheca)	⅛"	60-65 degrees	8-10	Important to germinate at cool soil temperature (below 70 degrees).
Ageratum	On surface	70-75 degrees	12-16	Fluorescent light will aid germination.
Alyssum	On surface	65-70 degrees	8-10	Water only with warm water.
Amaranthus	Cover lightly**	75-80 degrees	4-6	Keep soil temperature above 70 degrees for best germination.
Aster	⅛"-¼"	65-70 degrees	6-8	Grow wilt resistant varieties.
Balsam	On surface	70-75 degrees	6-8	Best germination at a constant soil temperature of 70 degrees.
Begonia, fibrous	On surface	70-75 degrees	16-20	Use dilute liquid feed when seedlings visible.
Browallia	On surface	70 degrees	12-14	Light will aid germination.
Calendula (Pot marigold)	¼"-½"	70 degrees	4-6	Keep seed covered with planting medium to exclude light.
Celosia (Cockscomb)	Cover lightly**	70 degrees	6-8	Seed is sensitive to drying out.
Coleus	On surface	70-75 degrees	10-12	Light needed for germination.
Dahlia	⅛"	65-70 degrees	8-12	Best germination with a constant 70 degree soil temperature.
Dianthus (annual)	Cover lightly**	70 degrees	6-12 (depending on variety)	Germinate perennial varieties at 75-80 degrees.
Gazania	⅛"-¼"	60 degrees	10-12	Exclude light for best germination.
Geranium (Hybrid)	⅛"	70-75 degrees	10-12	Germination temperature is critical.
Heliotrope	⅛"	70-75 degrees	10-12	Uniform soil temperature best for germination.
Impatiens	On surface	70-75 degrees	12-16	Fluorescent light aids germination. Do not expose to direct sunlight.
Lobelia	On surface	70-75 degrees	12-14	Water with warm water. Variety 'Heavenly' requires 50 degrees for germination.
Marigold	¼"	70-75 degrees	6-8	Dwarf marigolds are slower growing than taller varieties.
Nicotiana (Flowering tobacco)	On surface	70-75 degrees	6-8	Limit fertilizer to avoid leafy growth.
Petunia	On surface	70-80 degrees	10-12	Sow double varieties 2-4 weeks earlier.
Rudbeckia (perennial, Gloriosa daisy)	Cover lightly**	70-75 degrees	8-10	Will flower the first summer.
Salvia	On surface	70-75 degrees	8-10	Light aids germination.
Snapdragon	On surface	65-70 degrees	10-12	Pre-chill seed in refrigerator for a few days.
Verbena	¼"	65 degrees	8-10	Germinate in dark. Water the sowing medium one day before sowing.
Vinca (Periwinkle)	⅛"	70-75 degrees	12-14	Germinate in the dark. Sensitive to over watering.
Zinnias	⅛"-¼"	70-75 degrees	4-6	Sow as late as possible to avoid straggly growth.

Vegetables	Sowing Depth	Soil Temperature For Germination	Starting Time* (weeks before last killing frost)	Growing Tips
Broccoli	½"	65-70 degrees	4-6	Grow cool 55-60 degrees. Frost tolerant.
Brussels sprouts	½"	65-70 degrees	4-6	Grow cool 55-60 degrees. Frost tolerant.
Cabbage	½"	65-70 degrees	4-5	Grow cool 55-60 degrees. Frost tolerant.
Cauliflower	½"	65-70 degrees	5-6	Grow cool 55-60 degrees. Frost tolerant.
Cucumber	1"	70-75 degrees	3-5	Seed in a transplantable*** container. Frost sensitive.
Eggplant	¼"-½"	70-75 degrees	6-8	Frost sensitive.
Lettuce	¼"-½"	55-60 degrees	4-5	Grow cool 55-60 degrees.
Muskmelon	1"	75-80 degrees	3-5	Seed in a transplantable*** container. Frost sensitive.
Onion	½"	65-70 degrees	6-8	Very frost tolerant.
Pepper	¼"-½"	75-80 degrees	6-8	Frost sensitive.
Tomato	½"	75-80 degrees	6-8	Frost sensitive.
Watermelon Regular	1"	75-80 degrees	4-5	Frost sensitive. Seed in a transplantable*** container.
Watermelon Seedless	1"	75-80 degrees	5-6	

*Check with the local weather bureau or your County Agricultural Agent for the last spring frost date in your area.
**Lightly press the seeds into the medium surface.   ***Such as peat pots.
NOTE: Thoroughly mist sown containers or moisten by placing them in water. Cover, after draining, with a polyethylene bag, plastic wrap, waxed paper, or with clear glass. Remove covering as soon as seeds have sprouted.

PLANT SELECTION GUIDE

The charts on the following nine pages can be used as a quick guide to selecting the proper environment for a plant once you get it home.

The charts starting on the following page should be used as a guideline only. Higher humidity with good air circulation, for example, can permit admission of more intense light than the charts might indicate, but extremely low humidity with still air could sharply drop the tolerance level. Always make changes in a plant's environment progressively, moving one step at a time from low light intensity to bright, direct light. If a sudden adverse change results, take one step back and allow the plant a longer period of acclimation before trying the next rung on the ladder to a higher light intensity. Some of the figs, in particular, will end up as a bare stem, but don't be discouraged and don't throw the "dead" plant out. More often than not, new leaves will appear on the plant in a few days. Avoiding sudden changes in light level will go a long way toward preventing this problem. Also note that many plants are satisfied with a fairly wide range in light, exposure, and temperature requirements.

Defining the Categories

Exposures: *North*—a "window" facing north or more north than any other direction. *East*—a "window" facing east or more east than any other direction. *West*—a "window" facing west or more west than any other direction. *South*—a "window" facing south or more south than any other direction. For more detailed information on exposures, see pages 50-57.

Light requirement: *Direct sun*—sunlight falls directly on the plant for as long as 4-6 hours per day; above 800 f.c. *Winter direct sun*—sunlight falls directly on the plant in winter only. *Bright*—no direct sunlight on the plant, but intense indirect or filtered sunlight; 400-800 f.c. *Moderate*—an intermediate amount of light; 250-400 f.c. *Low*—a low amount of light, generally away from windows; 100-250 f.c. *Very low*—the lowest amount of light any plant can stand and still survive; 50-100 f.c.

Water requirements: *Keep wet at all times*—never allow the plant to dry out. Keep standing in saucer of wet gravel, changing every few days to avoid stagnation. *Keep evenly moist*—growing medium remains nicely moist to the touch, never oozing with water nor dusty dry. *Approach dryness between waterings*—soaking the rootball, then allowing soil to begin to feel dry to the touch before repeating soaking. *Dry out between waterings*—periods of soaking between which the soil should be allowed to become completely dry.

Humidity: *Average house*—30-45 percent. *Moist*—45-60 percent. *Very moist*—above 60 percent.

Temperature: *Cool*—Day 55-60° F. (13-15° C.). Night—40-50° F. (5-7° C.) *Average house*—Day—70° F. (21° C.) or slightly above. Night—50-55° F. (10-13° C.). *Warm*—Day—80-85° F. (27-30° C.). Night—62-65° F. (16-18° C.).

COMMON NAME	BOTANICAL NAME	Direct sun	Winter direct sun	Bright	Moderate	Low	Very low	North	East	West	South	Keep wet at all times	Keep evenly moist	Approach dryness between waterings	Dry out between waterings	Average house (hum.)	Moist	Very moist	Cool	Average house (temp.)	Warm	Foliage	Flowers	Fruit
Achimenes, Rainbow flower	*Achimenes* species	•		•					•	•	•		•				•			•			•	
Acidanthera	*Acidanthera* species	•		•							•			•		•			•	•			•	
African violets	*Saintpaulia* species		•	•	•				•	•			•				•			•		•	•	
Agapanthus	*Agapanthus* species	•		•	•				•	•	•		•				•		•	•			•	
Allamanda	*Allamanda* species	•							•	•	•		•				•			•		•	•	
Aluminum plant	*Pilea cadierei*			•	•				•	•			•				•			•		•		
Amaryllis	*Hippeastrum* species	•		•					•	•	•		•				•			•			•	
Amazon lily	*Eucharis grandiflora*		•	•					•	•	•		•				•			•			•	
Annuals and Vegetables	Many species	•							•	•	•		•			•				•	•	•	•	•
Anthurium, Flamingo flower	*Anthurium* species			•	•				•				•					•		•		•	•	
Aptenia	*Aptenia cordifolia*	•	•	•							•				•	•	•			•		•	•	
Arabian violet, German violet	*Exacum affine*			•	•				•				•				•			•			•	
Aralia	*Fatsia japonica*			•	•				•	•	•		•				•		•	•		•		
Aralia, false	*Dizygotheca elegantissima*			•	•			•	•				•				•			•		•		
Aralia, Ming	*Polyscias* species			•	•	•			•	•	•		•				•	•	•	•		•		
Ardisia, Coral berry	*Ardisia* species			•					•	•			•				•			•		•		•
Arrowhead	*Syngonium* species				•	•	•	•	•				•			•				•		•		
Artillery plant	*Pilea microphylla*			•					•	•			•				•			•		•		
Asparagus fern	*Asparagus* species			•	•	•		•	•	•	•		•				•			•		•		
Aspidistra	*Aspidistra elatior*			•	•	•	•		•	•			•			•				•		•		
Aucuba	*Aucuba japonica*			•	•				•	•			•			•				•		•		
Avocado	*Persea americana*	•		•					•	•	•		•				•			•		•		
Azalea	*Rhododendron* species			•					•		•		•				•	•	•				•	
Aztec lily, Jacobean lily	*Sprekelia formosissima*	•								•	•			•		•					•		•	
Baby's tears	*Soleirolia soleirolii*				•	•		•	•				•				•	•	•	•		•		
Banana	*Musa* species		•						•	•	•	•					•			•	•	•		
Barbados cherry	*Malpighia glabra*	•							•	•					•	•				•			•	
Basket vine	*Aeschynanthus* species			•					•	•			•				•			•			•	
Begonia (fibrous rooted)	*Begonia* species			•					•	•			•				•			•			•	
Rex	*Begonia rex-cultorum*			•	•				•	•			•				•			•		•		
Wax	*Begonia semperflorens*	•							•	•			•				•			•		•	•	
Bird of paradise	*Strelitzia* species	•		•						•	•		•				•			•			•	
Black-eyed Susan vine	*Thunbergia alata*	•							•	•			•			•				•			•	
Bleeding heart	*Clerodendron thomsoniae*																							
Blood lily	*Haemanthus* species	•		•					•		•		•				•			•			•	
Bougainvillea	*Bougainvillea* species	•								•	•		•				•			•			•	
Boxwood	*Buxus* species	•	•	•	•				•	•					•	•			•	•		•		
Braissaia, see Schefflera																								
Brazilian edelweiss	*Sinningia leucotricha*		•								•			•			•				•		•	•	
Bromeliads: Earth stars	*Cryptanthus* species			•	•				•	•			•				•	•		•		•		

COMMON NAME	BOTANICAL NAME	Direct sun	Winter direct sun	Bright	Moderate	Low	Very low	North	East	West	South	Keep wet at all times	Keep evenly moist	Approach dryness between waterings	Dry out between waterings	Average house (humidity)	Moist	Very moist	Cool	Average house (temp)	Warm	Foliage	Flowers	Fruit
Fingernail plant	*Neoregelia* species		•	•					•	•			•			•	•			•		•		
Flaming sword	*Vriesea* species			•	•				•	•			•	•			•			•		•	•	
Grecian vase	*Quesnelia* species			•					•	•			•				•			•		•	•	
Living vase plant	*Aechmea* species			•					•	•			•				•			•		•	•	
Pineapple	*Ananas* species	•								•	•		•				•	•		•		•		•
Queen's Tears	*Billbergia* species		•	•					•	•			•				•			•		•	•	
Volcano plant	*Bromelia* species	•								•			•				•			•		•		•
No common name	*Catopsis* species	•									•	•					•			•		•		
No common name	*Dyckia* species			•	•				•	•				•			•			•		•		
No common name	*Guzmania* species		•						•		•		•				•			•		•	•	
No common name	*Nidularium* species			•					•	•			•				•				•	•		
No common name	*Portea* species	•		•	•				•	•				•			•				•	•	•	
No common name	*Tillandsia* species	•		•					•	•					•		•					•		
Butterfly gardenia	*Tabernaemontana divericata*	•							•	•			•			•				•			•	
Cacti:																								
Ball cactus	*Notocactus* species	•		•					•	•			•			•				•			•	•
Barrel cactus	*Echinopsis* species	•		•					•	•			•		•	•				•			•	•
Barrel cactus, Star	*Echinocactus* species	•		•					•	•			•			•				•			•	
Bishop's cap	*Astrophytum* species	•		•					•	•			•			•				•			•	
Bunny ears	*Opuntia* species	•		•					•	•			•			•				•			•	•
Chin cactus	*Gymnocalycium* species	•		•					•	•			•			•				•			•	
Christmas cactus	*Schlumbergera* species			•	•			•	•	•		•					•			•			•	
Cob cactus	*Lobivia* species	•		•					•	•			•			•				•			•	
Column, Torch	*Cleistocactus* species	•		•					•	•			•			•				•			•	
Crown cactus	*Rebutia* species	•		•					•	•			•			•				•			•	
Lemon vine	*Pereskia* species	•		•					•	•			•			•				•			•	
Mistletoe cactus	*Rhipsalis* species			•	•			•	•				•				•			•		•	•	•
Night-blooming cactus	*Hylocereus* species			•	•			•	•	•	•		•				•				•	•	•	
Old man cactus	*Cephalocereus* species	•							•	•			•			•				•		•		
Orchid cactus	*Epiphyllum* species			•	•				•	•	•		•				•			•			•	
Peanut cactus	*Chamaecereus sylvestri*	•	•	•					•	•	•			•		•			•	•			•	
Pincushion	*Mammillaria* species	•		•					•	•			•			•				•			•	
Rainbow cactus, Hedgehog	*Echinocereus* species	•		•					•	•				•		•				•			•	•
Rat-tail cactus	*Aporocactus* species	•		•					•	•			•			•				•			•	
Thanksgiving cactus	*Schlumbergera* species			•	•			•	•	•		•					•			•			•	
No common name	*Cereus* species	•		•					•	•			•			•				•		•	•	•
Caladium	*Caladium* species			•	•			•	•	•			•				•				•	•		
Calceolaria	*Calceolaria* species			•	•			•	•				•				•		•				•	
Calico flower	*Aristolochia* species			•					•	•			•			•				•			•	
Calla lily	*Zantedeschia* species	•							•	•	•	•					•			•			•	
Camellia	*Camellia* species			•					•	•			•				•		•	•		•	•	
Campanula, Star-of-Bethlehem	*Campanula* species			•					•	•			•			•				•			•	

COMMON NAME	BOTANICAL NAME	Direct sun	Winter direct sun	Bright	Moderate	Low	Very low	North	East	West	South	Keep wet at all times	Keep evenly moist	Approach dryness between waterings	Dry out between waterings	Average house	Moist	Very moist	Cool	Average house	Warm	Foliage	Flowers	Fruit
		LIGHT REQUIREMENTS						EXPOSURE				WATER REQUIREMENTS				HUMIDITY			TEMPERATURE			MOST ATTRACTIVE FEATURES		
Candle plant	Plectranthus oertendahlii			•				•	•				•				•			•		•	•	
Cape primrose	Streptocarpus species	•		•				•	•	•				•		•				•			•	
Cardinal flower	Sinningia cardinalis			•					•	•				•						•			•	
Carolina jasmine	Gelsemium sempervirens			•				•	•				•				•			•			•	
Chenille plant	Acalypha hispida	•						•	•	•			•			•				•			•	
Chincherinchee	Ornithogalum thyrsoides	•		•					•		•				•	•			•				•	
Chinese evergreen	Aglaonema species			•	•	•	•	•	•			•					•			•		•		
Chrysanthemum	Chrysanthemum species			•					•					•		•			•				•	
Cigar plant	Cuphea ignea	•		•				•	•	•			•							•		•	•	
Cineraria	Senecio hybridus			•	•				•	•			•						•				•	
Clubmoss	Selaginella species				•			•	•				•				•			•		•		
Citrus:																								
Calamondin	Citrofortunella mitis	•							•	•			•			•				•		•		•
Kumquat	Fortunella margarita	•							•	•			•			•				•		•		•
Meyer lemon	Citrus limon 'Meyer'	•							•	•	•		•			•				•		•		•
Otaheite orange	Citrus taitensis	•							•	•			•			•				•		•		•
Sweet orange	Citrus sinensis	•							•	•			•			•				•		•		•
Tangerine, Satsuma orange	Citrus reticulata	•							•	•			•			•				•		•		•
Wonder lemon	Citrus limon 'Ponderosa'	•							•	•	•		•			•				•		•		•
Clerodendrum	Clerodendrum species			•				•	•	•			•			•	•			•		•	•	
Clivia	Clivia species			•					•	•			•			•			•	•			•	
Coffee	Coffea species			•					•	•	•		•				•			•		•		
Coleus	Coleus species	•		•	•				•	•			•			•				•		•		
Columnea	Columnea species			•					•	•			•				•	•		•			•	
Copperleaf	Acalypha wilkesiana	•		•					•				•			•				•		•		
Coral plant	Russelia equisetiformis	•							•						•	•				•			•	
Corn lily	Ixia species	•		•					•	•					•	•			•				•	
Creeping Charlie	Pilea nummulariifolia				•			•	•	•			•				•			•		•		
Creeping fig, see Figs																								
Crinum	Crinum species		•	•				•	•	•			•				•			•		•	•	
Crocus	Crocus species	•							•		•		•			•			•				•	
Crossandra, Firecracker flower	Crossandra infundibuliformis		•						•	•			•				•			•			•	
Croton	Codiaeum species	•							•				•			•				•		•		
Cup-and-saucer vine	Cobaea scandens			•					•		•		•				•			•		•	•	
Cycas	Cycas species	•		•				•	•	•			•			•				•		•		
Cyclamen	Cyclamen species			•					•				•				•	•		•			•	•
Cyperus	Cyperus species		•	•					•	•	•	•				•			•					
Daffodils	Narcissus species			•					•	•	•		•				•		•				•	
Devil's backbone	Pedilanthus tithymaloides			•	•			•	•	•			•				•			•		•		
Dieffenbachia	Dieffenbachia species			•	•	•		•						•		•				•		•		
Double decker plant	Sinningia verticillata		•						•	•				•		•				•			•	

COMMON NAME	BOTANICAL NAME	Direct sun	Winter direct sun	Bright	Moderate	Low	Very low	North	East	West	South	Keep wet at all times	Keep evenly moist	Approach dryness between waterings	Dry out between waterings	Average house	Moist	Very moist	Cool	Average house	Warm	Foliage	Flowers	Fruit
		LIGHT REQUIREMENTS						EXPOSURE				WATER REQUIREMENTS				HUMIDITY			TEMPERATURE			MOST ATTRACTIVE FEATURES		
Dracaena	*Dracaena* species			•	•	•	•	•	•			•					•			•		•		
Dragon tree	*Dracaena draco*	•	•	•	•				•	•	•			•		•				•		•		
Easter lily	*Lilium longiflorum*			•					•	•				•		•			•				•	
Egyptian star flower	*Pentas lanceolata*	•							•	•	•		•			•					•		•	
Elaeagnus	*Elaeagnus* species	•	•	•					•	•	•			•		•				•		•		
Elephant ears	*Colocasia* species			•					•	•	•	•					•				•	•		
Episcia	*Episcia* species			•	•				•	•	•		•				•				•		•	
Euonymus (evergreen)	*Euonymus japonica*			•					•	•			•			•			•	•		•		
False sea onion	*Ornithogalum caudatum*	•		•					•	•	•				•	•							•	
Felicia, Blue Marguerite	*Felicia amelioides*	•		•					•	•	•					•							•	
Ferns: Bear's paw	*Aglaomorpha meyeniana*	•						•	•				•			•				•		•		
Bird's nest	*Asplenium nidus*				•	•		•	•				•				•			•		•		
Boston	*Nephrolepis exaltata* 'Bostoniensis'				•	•		•	•				•				•			•		•		
Brake ferns	*Pteris* species	•	•	•	•								•						•	•		•		
Deersfoot	*Davallia canariensis*				•			•	•				•				•	•	•			•		
Fluffy ruffles	*Nephrolepis exaltata* 'Fluffy Ruffles'				•	•		•	•				•				•			•		•		
Hare's foot	*Polypodium aureum*	•	•	•					•		•		•				•			•		•		
Hart's tongue	*Phyllitis scolopendrium*				•	•			•				•				•			•		•		
Hawaiian tree	*Cibotium chamissoi*				•				•				•				•			•		•		
Holly fern	*Cyrtomium falcatum*	•	•	•	•	•		•	•				•				•			•		•		
Maidenhair	*Adiantum* species			•	•	•		•	•				•	•			•	•		•		•		
Mother	*Asplenium bulbiferum*			•	•	•			•				•				•			•		•		
Rabbit's foot	*Davallia fejeensis*			•	•	•			•				•				•	•	•			•		
Squirrel's foot, Ballfern	*Davallia mariesii*			•	•	•			•				•				•	•				•		
Staghorn	*Platycerium* species			•	•				•	•			•				•			•		•		
Treefern	*Cibotium* species			•					•				•				•			•		•		
Treefern	*Alsophila* species		•	•					•	•	•	•					•				•	•		
Treefern	*Cyathea* species			•					•	•	•	•					•				•	•		
Trembling brake	*Pteris tremula*			•	•			•	•				•				•	•	•			•		
Whitman	*Nephrolepis exaltata* 'Whitmanii'			•	•			•	•				•				•			•		•		
Figs: Creeping	*Ficus pumila*			•	•				•	•			•				•			•		•		
Fiddle-leaf	*Ficus lyrata*			•	•				•	•			•			•	•			•		•		
Indian laurel	*Ficus retusa*			•	•				•	•			•				•			•		•		
Mistletoe	*Ficus deltoidea*			•	•				•	•			•			•				•		•		•
Rubber plant	*Ficus elastica*			•	•	•		•	•	•	•		•			•	•			•		•		
Weeping	*Ficus benjamina*			•	•				•	•	•		•				•			•		•		
Firecracker vine	*Manettia cordifolia*			•					•				•			•				•			•	
Fittonia	*Fittonia* species				•			•	•				•				•	•	•			•		

COMMON NAME	BOTANICAL NAME	Direct sun	Winter direct sun	Bright	Moderate	Low	Very low	North	East	West	South	Keep wet at all times	Keep evenly moist	Approach dryness between waterings	Dry out between waterings	Average house	Moist	Very moist	Cool	Average house	Warm	Foliage	Flowers	Fruit
		LIGHT REQUIREMENTS						EXPOSURE				WATER REQUIREMENTS				HUMIDITY			TEMPERATURE			MOST ATTRACTIVE FEATURES		
Flagplant (miniature)	*Acorus gramineus*				•	•		•	•			•					•	•				•		
Flowering maple	*Abutilon* species	•							•				•			•				•		•	•	
Freesia	*Freesia* species			•					•	•	•		•				•		•				•	
Fuchsia	*Fuchsia hybrida*			•					•	•			•				•		•			•	•	
Gardenia	*Gardenia jasminoides*		•						•				•				•			•		•	•	
Gazania	*Gazania* species	•		•					•	•	•			•			•			•			•	
Geranium	*Pelargonium* species	•		•					•	•	•			•		•	•			•			•	
Geranium (Ivy)	*Pelargonium peltatum*	•		•					•	•	•			•		•	•			•			•	
Glory lily	*Gloriosa* species	•		•					•	•	•		•				•			•			•	
Gloxinera	*Sinningia* species			•					•				•				•			•			•	
Gloxinia	*Sinningia* species			•	•				•				•				•			•			•	
Goldfish plant	*Nematanthus* species		•						•				•			•	•			•			•	
Goldust plant	*Aucuba japonica* 'Variegata'			•	•	•		•	•					•			•		•			•		
Grape-hyacinth	*Muscari* species	•		•					•	•	•	•	•				•		•				•	
Grape ivy	*Cissus rhombifolia*			•	•			•	•	•			•				•			•		•		
Grecian urn plant, Grecian pattern	*Acanthus* species			•					•	•			•			•				•			•	
Hawaiian ti	*Cordyline terminalis*			•	•	•		•	•				•				•			•		•		
Heath, Heather	*Erica* species			•					•				•				•		•				•	
Heliotrope	*Heliotropium arborescens*	•							•				•				•			•			•	
Hibiscus	*Hibiscus rosa-sinensis*	•		•					•				•				•			•			•	
Holly osmanthus	*Osmanthus* species	•		•					•	•			•				•			•		•		
Homalomena	*Homalomena* species				•	•			•				•				•				•	•		
Hyacinth	*Hyacinthus orientalis*	•		•	•				•				•				•		•				•	
Hydrangea	*Hydrangea macrophylla*	•		•					•		•	•	•			•			•				•	
Impatiens	*Impatiens* species		•	•					•	•				•				•		•			•	
Indoor oak	*Buddleia* species	•		•					•		•		•			•				•	•	•		
Iresine	*Iresine* species	•		•					•		•			•		•				•	•	•		
Ivy (Algerian)	*Hedera canariensis*	•		•					•	•	•		•			•				•		•		
Ivy (English)	*Hedera helix*			•				•	•	•			•			•	•			•		•		
Ixora	*Ixora* species	•		•					•	•			•				•			•			•	
Jasmine	*Cestrum, Jasminum* and *Gelsemium* species			•					•				•			•	•		•	•		•	•	
Jerusalem cherry, Christmas cherry	*Solanum pseudocapsicum*	•		•					•				•				•		•					•
Joseph's coat	*Alternathera* species	•		•						•			•			•				•		•		
Kangaroo vine, Kangaroo ivy	*Cissus antarctica*			•	•	•		•	•				•				•			•		•		
Kenilworth ivy	*Cymbalaria muralis*			•					•				•				•		•			•		
King's crown	*Justicia carnea*	•	•	•					•		•		•				•			•			•	
Kohleria	*Kohleria* species			•					•	•			•				•				•		•	
Lantana	*Lantana* species	•		•					•	•	•			•		•				•			•	
Lily-of-the-valley	*Convallaria majalis*	•							•	•		•				•			•				•	

Common Name	Botanical Name	Direct sun	Winter direct sun	Bright	Moderate	Low	Very low	North	East	West	South	Keep wet at all times	Keep evenly moist	Approach dryness between waterings	Dry out between waterings	Average house	Moist	Very moist	Cool	Average house	Warm	Foliage	Flowers	Fruit
Lily turf	*Liriope* and *Ophiopogon* species			•	•				•	•	•		•				•		•				•	
Lipstick vine	*Aeschynanthus* species			•					•		•		•				•	•		•			•	
Loquat	*Eriobotrya japonica*	•		•					•	•	•		•				•			•		•		
Love plant	*Medinilla magnifica*			•	•				•	•			•				•				•		•	
Mandevilla	*Mandevilla* species	•		•					•	•	•				•		•	•		•			•	
Marguerite	*Chrysanthemum frutescens*	•							•	•	•		•			•			•				•	
Mexican flame vine	*Senecio confusus*		•						•	•	•		•			•			•				•	
Mexican foxglove	*Tetranema roseum*		•						•	•			•			•				•			•	
Monkey puzzle	*Araucaria araucana*			•					•		•		•				•			•		•		
Monstera	*Monstera* species				•	•		•	•	•	•		•			•	•			•		•		
Montbretia	*Crocosmia* species	•		•					•	•	•			•		•				•			•	
Morning glory	*Ipomoea* species	•		•					•	•	•		•				•			•			•	
Moses in the cradle	*Rhoeo* species			•	•				•	•	•		•			•				•		•		
Myrtle	*Myrtus communis*	•		•					•	•	•			•		•			•			•	•	
Nandina, Heavenly bamboo	*Nandina domestica*	•		•					•	•	•		•				•		•			•	•	
Narcissus	*Narcissus* species	•		•					•	•	•		•				•		•				•	
Natal plum	*Carissa grandiflora*	•		•					•	•	•		•				•			•		•	•	•
Nerine	*Nerine, Lycoris* species	•		•					•		•			•		•			•				•	
Norfolk Island pine	*Araucaria heterophylla*			•	•	•		•	•	•			•				•		•	•		•		
Oleander	*Nerium oleander*	•		•					•	•	•		•				•			•			•	
Olive	*Olea europaea*	•		•					•	•	•			•		•	•		•			•		
Onion, Flowering	*Allium* species	•							•	•			•				•			•			•	
Orchids:																								
Carnival	*Ascocentrum* species	•							•				•				•				•		•	
Cattleya	*Cattleya* species	•							•					•				•		•			•	
Clamshell, Butterfly	*Epidendrum* species	•		•					•					•				•		•			•	
Comet	*Angraecum* species			•					•				•			•				•			•	
Cymbidium	*Cymbidium* species	•							•				•					•		•			•	
Dancing lady, Butterfly	*Oncidium* species	•		•					•				•					•		•			•	
Fox-brush	*Aerides* species	•							•						•			•		•			•	
Kite	*Masdevallia* species				•		•		•				•				•		•				•	
Lady-of-the-night	*Brassavola* species	•							•					•				•		•			•	
Lady slipper	*Paphiopedilum* species				•				•				•				•	•		•			•	
Lily-of-the-valley, Tiger	*Odontoglossum* species		•						•					•				•	•				•	
Moth	*Phalaenopsis* species			•					•				•				•			•			•	
Pansy	*Miltonia* species			•					•				•			•			•				•	
Punch and Judy	*Gongora* species			•					•					•						•			•	
Rodriguez	*Rodriguezia* species			•					•				•				•					•	•	
Spider	*Ansellia* species	•							•				•			•					•	•	
Vanda	*Vanda* species			•					•				•				•				•	•	

		LIGHT REQUIREMENTS						EXPOSURE				WATER REQUIREMENTS				HUMIDITY			TEMPERATURE			MOST ATTRACTIVE FEATURES		
COMMON NAME	BOTANICAL NAME	Direct sun	Winter direct sun	Bright	Moderate	Low	Very low	North	East	West	South	Keep wet at all times	Keep evenly moist	Approach dryness between waterings	Dry out between waterings	Average house	Moist	Very moist	Cool	Average house	Warm	Foliage	Flowers	Fruit
No common name	*Acineta* species	•							•				•				•				•		•	
No common name	*Bifrenaria* species			•	•			•	•				•				•				•		•	
No common name	*Coelogyne* species			•					•						•	•				•			•	
No common name	*Dendrobium* species			•						•	•		•			•				•			•	
No common name	*Laelia* species	•		•					•				•			•			•				•	
No common name	*Lycaste* species	•							•				•			•			•				•	
No common name	*Maxillaria* species			•					•								•		•				•	
No common name	*Neofinetia* species			•					•					•		•			•				•	
No common name	*Trichocentrum* species			•					•					•		•				•			•	
No common name	*Zygopetalum* species			•					•						•	•				•			•	
Oxalis	*Oxalis* species	•		•				•	•	•			•				•			•		•		
Palms:																								
Areca, Butterfly	*Chrysalidocarpus lutescens*			•	•				•				•		•	•				•		•		
Bamboo	*Chamaedorea* species				•	•			•				•		•	•				•		•		
Chinese fan	*Livistona chinensis*			•					•	•			•				•			•		•		
Dwarf date	*Phoenix roebelenii*			•	•				•				•			•				•		•		
European fan	*Chamaerops humilis*	•		•					•	•	•		•			•			•			•		
Fishtail	*Caryota* species			•					•				•	•	•		•				•	•		
Kentia, Paradise, Sentry	*Howea* species			•	•	•		•	•	•	•		•			•				•		•		
Lady	*Rhapis* species			•				•	•				•			•				•		•		
Manila	*Veitchia merrillii*			•					•	•	•		•				•				•	•		
Parlor, Dwarf mountain	*Chamaedorea elegans*				•	•	•	•	•						•						•	•		
Tufted or clustered fishtail	*Caryota mitis*			•				•	•				•				•				•	•		
Pan American friendship plant, Panamiga	*Pilea involucrata*				•			•	•				•			•	•			•		•		
Papyrus	*Cyperus* species	•		•				•	•	•	•						•			•		•		
Parlor ivy, German ivy	*Senecio mikanioides*		•					•	•	•			•				•		•			•	•	
Parrot flower	*Heliconia psittacorum*	•						•	•	•			•				•				•		•	
Passion flower	*Passiflora* species	•		•					•	•			•				•			•			•	
Peace lily	*Spathiphyllum* species			•	•	•		•	•				•				•				•	•	•	
Peacock plant	*Calathea* species			•	•			•	•				•				•				•	•		
Pellionia	*Pellionia*				•	•		•	•	•			•				•				•	•		
Peperomia	*Peperomia* species				•			•	•	•					•		•			•		•		
Pepper	*Capsicum* species	•		•				•			•		•				•				•		•	•
Philodendron	*Philodendron* species				•	•	•	•	•	•			•			•	•			•		•		
Piggyback plant	*Tolmiea menziesii*			•	•	•		•	•				•				•			•		•		
Pineapple lily	*Eucomis* species			•				•	•	•			•				•			•			•	
Pittosporum	*Pittosporum tobira*	•		•				•	•				•				•		•			•	•	
Pleomele	*Dracaena* species			•	•	•		•	•			•					•				•	•		
Plumbago	*Plumbago* species	•		•				•	•	•			•				•			•		•	•	
Podocarpus	*Podocarpus* species		•	•					•		•		•				•			•		•		
Poinsettia	*Euphorbia pulcherrima*	•	•	•					•		•		•			•				•			•	
Polka dot plant	*Hypoestes phyllostachya*	•		•					•		•		•				•				•	•		

COMMON NAME	BOTANICAL NAME	Direct sun	Winter direct sun	Bright	Moderate	Low	Very low	North	East	West	South	Keep wet at all times	Keep evenly moist	Approach dryness between waterings	Dry out between waterings	Average house	Moist	Very moist	Cool	Average house	Warm	Foliage	Flowers	Fruit
		LIGHT REQUIREMENTS						EXPOSURE				WATER REQUIRE-MENTS				HUMIDITY			TEMPERA-TURE			MOST ATTRACTIVE FEATURES		
Pomegranate	*Punica granatum*	●		●						●	●		●				●			●				●
Ponytail palm	*Beaucarnea recurvata*	●		●	●				●	●	●			●		●				●		●		
Pothos, Devil's ivy	*Epipremnun* and *Scindapsus* species			●	●	●	●	●	●				●				●			●		●		
Powder puff	*Calliandra* species	●		●					●	●	●		●				●				●		●	
Prayer plant	*Maranta* species				●			●	●				●				●			●		●		
Princess flower	*Tibouchina urvilleana*	●	●	●					●	●	●		●			●			●	●			●	
Privet	*Ligustrum* species	●		●					●	●	●		●				●			●		●		
Purple heart	*Setcreasea purpurea*			●					●		●			●			●			●		●		
Purple velvet plant	*Gynura scandens*			●	●				●	●			●				●			●		●		
Pyracantha	*Pyracantha* species	●	●	●					●	●	●			●		●			●	●				●
Queen's wreath	*Petrea volubilis*	●									●	●	●				●			●			●	
Rain lily	*Zephyranthes* species	●		●					●			●					●			●			●	
Rhododendron	*Rhododendron* species		●	●	●			●	●	●	●		●			●	●		●				●	
Ranunculus	*Ranunculus asiaticus*	●	●	●					●	●	●		●			●			●				●	
Rice-paper plant	*Tetrapanax papyriferus*	●		●					●	●	●		●				●			●		●		
Rosary vine	*Ceropegia woodii*	●		●					●	●	●				●	●				●		●		
Rose (miniature)	*Rosa* species	●		●					●	●	●		●				●			●			●	
Rosemary	*Rosmarinus officinalis*	●		●					●	●	●			●			●			●		●	●	
Ruellia	*Ruellia* species			●					●	●			●				●			●			●	
Sage (Blue)	*Eranthemum pulchellum*				●				●	●	●		●				●				●		●	
Sage (Scarlet)	*Salvia* species	●		●					●	●	●		●				●			●			●	
Sapphire flower	*Browallia speciosa* 'Major'	●							●	●	●		●			●				●			●	
Scarborough-lily	*Vallota speciosa*	●		●					●		●		●				●			●			●	
Schefflera	*Schefflera* and *Brassaia* species			●					●	●	●			●			●			●		●		
Screw pine	*Pandanus* species			●	●			●	●				●				●	●		●		●		
Sea grape	*Coccoloba uvifera*			●					●		●		●			●				●		●		
Seersucker plant	*Geogenanthus undatus*			●					●		●		●				●				●	●		
Shrimp plant	*Justicia brandegeana*	●		●					●	●	●				●		●			●			●	●
Silk oak	*Grevillea robusta*	●		●					●	●	●			●			●			●		●		
Singapore holly	*Malpighia coccigera*	●		●							●		●				●			●			●	
Slipperwort, see Calceolaria																								
Snake plant	*Sansevieria* species	●		●	●	●	●	●	●	●	●			●			●			●		●		
Society garlic	*Tulbaghia violacea*			●					●		●	●					●			●		●	●	
Spanish shawl	*Heterocentron elegans*	●		●					●	●	●	●					●			●			●	
Spiderplant	*Chlorophytum* species			●	●			●	●	●	●		●				●			●		●		
Squills	*Scilla* species	●		●					●				●			●			●				●	
Star-jasmine	*Trachelospermum jasminoides*		●						●	●				●			●			●		●	●	
Star-of-Bethlehem	*Ornithogalum* species	●		●					●	●	●			●		●			●				●	
Stephanotis	*Stephanotis floribunda*	●							●		●		●				●			●			●	
Stepladder plant	*Costus malortieanus*			●	●				●	●			●				●				●	●		

COMMON NAME	BOTANICAL NAME	LIGHT REQUIREMENTS						EXPOSURE				WATER REQUIREMENTS				HUMIDITY			TEMPERATURE			MOST ATTRACTIVE FEATURES		
		Direct sun	Winter direct sun	Bright	Moderate	Low	Very low	North	East	West	South	Keep wet at all times	Keep evenly moist	Approach dryness between waterings	Dry out between waterings	Average house	Moist	Very moist	Cool	Average house	Warm	Foliage	Flowers	Fruit
Strawberry geranium	*Saxifraga stolonifera*			●	●			●	●				●	●			●			●		●		
Streptosolen	*Streptosolen jamesonii*		●	●					●		●		●				●			●		●	●	
String-of-pearls	*Senecio rowleyanus*			●					●		●		●				●		●				●	
Succulents: Adromischus	*Adromischus* species	●	●	●							●			●	●	●	●			●		●		
Baby toes	*Fenestraria* species	●		●					●	●				●	●	●	●			●		●		
Century plant	*Agave* species	●							●	●				●	●	●	●			●		●		
Climbing onion	*Bowiea volubillis*			●	●				●	●			●			●	●			●		●		
Crown of thorns	*Euphorbia millii*	●		●					●	●				●	●	●	●			●			●	
Donkey's tail, Coral beads	*Sedum* species	●		●					●	●	●			●	●	●	●			●		●		
Ice plant	*Aptenia* and other genera	●							●	●			●			●	●			●			●	
Living stones, Stone face	*Lithops* and other genera	●							●	●				●	●	●	●			●		●	●	
Moonstones	*Pachyphytum* species	●		●					●	●	●			●	●	●	●			●		●	●	
Ox-tongue	*Gasteria* species			●	●				●	●			●			●				●		●		
Propeller, Rattlesnake, Scarlet paintbrush	*Crassula* species	●		●					●	●	●		●	●		●	●			●		●		
Starfish flower	*Stapelia* species	●		●					●	●	●		●			●	●			●			●	
Tiger jaws	*Faucaria* species	●							●	●				●	●	●	●			●		●		
Zebra, Wart	*Haworthia* species	●							●	●				●	●	●	●			●		●		
No common name	*Aloe* species	●		●					●	●			●			●				●		●	●	
No common name	*Echeveria* species	●		●					●	●				●	●	●				●		●	●	
No common name	*Kalanchoe* species	●		●					●	●	●			●	●	●	●		●	●		●	●	
Swedish ivy	*Plectranthus* species			●	●				●	●	●		●				●			●		●		
Sweet olive	*Osmanthus fragrans*	●		●					●	●	●		●				●		●	●		●		
Taffeta plant	*Hoffmannia* species				●			●	●				●				●			●		●		
Temple bells	*Smithiantha* species			●	●				●		●		●				●				●	●		
Tree ivy	*Fatshedera lizei*	●		●	●			●	●	●	●		●				●		●	●		●		
Treevine, Begonia Cissus	*Cissus discolor*			●	●				●		●		●				●			●		●		
Tulips	*Tulipa* species			●					●	●	●		●			●			●				●	
Turk's cap	*Malvaviscus arboreus*	●		●					●	●	●		●			●			●				●	
Veltheimia	*Veltheimia* species			●					●				●				●		●			●		
	Cyanotis species		●	●	●				●	●	●			●		●				●		●		
	Gibasis species			●	●			●	●				●			●				●		●		
Wandering Jew	*Setcreasea* species		●	●	●			●	●					●		●	●			●		●		
	Tradescantia species			●	●				●					●	●		●			●		●		
	Zebrina species			●	●				●				●				●			●		●		
Wand flower	*Sparaxis* species	●		●					●	●	●		●			●			●				●	
Wax plant	*Hoya* species	●		●	●				●	●			●			●				●			●	
Winter creeper	*Euonymus radicans*			●						●	●		●				●			●		●		
Wire plant	*Muehlenbeckia* species	●		●					●	●			●				●			●		●		
Yucca	*Yucca* species	●		●					●	●	●				●		●			●		●	●	
Zebra plant	*Aphelandra* species			●					●	●			●			●				●		●	●	
Zephyr lily	*Zephyranthes* species	●		●					●	●	●						●			●			●	

Plant Resources

Only a few years ago, most of us who wanted a container plant that was the least bit unusual had to send away for it from a specialist. Because of plant popularity and mass dissemination of rare species and new varieties, this is all changing today. More and more local garden centers and plant shops offer the choice, the offbeat, the truly exotic. However, there are certain special plants available only from highly specialized suppliers, and for that reason we list these growers here, along with mailing addresses and an indication of any charges made for catalogs. It is also true that some people who live away from population centers may need to order all plants and supplies by mail.

Sources for Plants

Abbey Garden
P.O. Box 30331, Santa Barbara, CA 93105
Cacti and other succulents.
Catalog $1.00.

Abbot's Nursery
Route 4, Box 482, Mobile, AL 36009
Camellias.

Alberts & Merkel Brothers
2210 South Federal Highway
Boynton Beach, FL 33435
Orchids and other tropicals.
Catalog $1.00.

Antonelli Brothers
2545 Capitola Road, Santa Cruz,
CA 95010
Tuberous begonias, gloxinias, achimenes.

Ashcroft Orchids
19062 Ballinger Way N.E., Seattle 55, WA
Botanical orchids.

Bart's Nursery
522 Fifth Street, Fullerton, PA 18052
Bonsai materials.

Buell's Greenhouse
P.O. Box 218 HPC, Weeks Road
Eastford, CT 06242
African violets, gloxinias, other gesneriads.
Descriptive list 25¢ plus 28¢ SASE.

Burgess Seed and Plant Company
Galesburg, MI 49053
Dwarf fruit, other houseplants.

Burnett Brothers, Inc.
92 Chambers Street, NY 10007
Freesias and other bulbous plants.

Burpee, W. Atlee, Company
Warminster, PA 18974
Seeds, bulbs, supplies.

Cook's Geranium Nursery
712 North Grand, Lyons, KS 67544
Geraniums. Catalog 50¢.

De Giorgi Company, Inc.
Council Bluffs, IA 51504
Seeds and bulbs.

De Jager, P., and Sons, Inc.
188 Asbury Street, South Hamilton,
MA 01982
Bulbs for forcing.

Farmer Seed and Nursery Company
Faribault, MN 55021
Dwarf citrus and other houseplants.

Fennell Orchid Company
26715 S.W. 157 Avenue, Homestead,
FL 33032
Orchids and other indoor specialities.

Field, Henry, Seed and Nursery Company
Shenandoah, IA 51601
Houseplants and supplies.

Fischer Greenhouses
Linwood, NJ
African violets and other gesneriads; supplies for growing houseplants.

Green Acres Nursery
14451 N.E. Second Street, North Miami, FL 33161
Palms.

Orchids by Hausermann, Ind.
P.O. Box 363, Elmhurst, IL 60126
Unusual species orchids.

Hilltop Herb Farm
P.O. Box 1734, Cleveland, TX 77327
Herbs and herb products.

Jones and Scully, Inc.
2200 N.E. 33rd Avenue, Miami, FL 33142
Orchids and other tropicals.

Kartuz, Michael J.
92 Chestnut Street, Wilmington, MA 01887
Houseplants, many bred specifically for fluorescent-light culture. Catalog 50¢.

Logee's Greenhouses
55 North Street, Danielson, CT 06239
All kinds of houseplants including rare and unusual exotics. Catalog $2.00.

Lyon, Lyndon
14 Mutchler Street, Dolgeville, NY 13329
African violets, gesneriads.

McClellan, Rod, Company
1450 El Camino Real,
South San Francisco, CA 94080
Orchids and supplies for growing.

Merry Gardens
P.O. Box 595, Camden, ME 04843
Houseplants for cool climates and herbs. List 50¢.

Mini-Roses
Box 4255 Station A, Dallas, TX 75208
Miniature roses.

Nies Nursery
5710 S.W. 37th Street, West Hollywood, FL 33023
Palms.

Nuccio's Nurseries
3555 Chaney Trail, Altadena, CA 91002
Camellias.

Park, George W., Seed Co., Inc.
Greenwood, SC 29647
All kinds of houseplants, seeds, bulbs, fluorescent lighting equipment, other supplies.

Sequoia Nursery
2519 East Noble Avenue, Visalia, CA 93277
Miniature roses, including basket and moss types.

Stewart, Fred A., Inc.
1212 East Las Tunas Drive, San Gabriel, CA 91778
Orchids and supplies for growing.

Sunnybrook Farms
P.O. Box 6, 9448 Mayfield Road
Chesterland, OH 44026
Herbs, houseplants, perennials, geraniums, cactus and succulents.

Tinari Greenhouses
2325 Valley Road, Huntington Valley, PA 19006

African violet specialist, supplies and lighting equipment. Color catalog 25¢.

Wilson Brothers
Roachdale, IN 46172
Geraniums and other houseplants.

Yoshimura Bonsai Company, Inc.
200 Benedict Avenue, Tarrytown, NY 10591
Bonsai and supplies.

Sources for Fluorescent Lighting Equipment

Craft-House Manufacturing Company
Wilson, NY 10706
Lighted plant stands.

Floralite Company
4124 East Oakwood Road, Oak Creek WI 53221
Fluorescent fixtures, mist sprayers, tubes, timers, trays, labels, other equipment and growing supplies.

General Electric Company
Lamp Division, Nela Park, Cleveland, OH
Manufacturers of fluorescent and incandescent lamps.

Sylvania Electric Products, Inc.
60 Boston Street, Salem, MA 01971
Manufacturers of all types of fluorescent lamps, including growth lamps.

Tube Craft, Inc.
8000 Baker Avenue, Cleveland, OH 44102
FloraCart and other lighting equipment and supplies.

Westinghouse Electric Corporation
Westinghouse Lamp Division,
Bloomfield, NJ.
Manufacturers of fluorescent lamps.

Sources for Home Greenhouses

Aluminum Greenhouses, Inc.
14615 Lorain Avenue, Cleveland, OH 44111.

Geodesic Domes
R.R. 1, Bloomington, IL 61701.

J. A. Nearing Co., Inc.
10788 Tucker Street, Beltsville, MD 20705

Lord & Burnham
Irvington, New York, NY 10533.

Redwood Domes
2664 Highway 1, Aptos, CA 95003.

Peter Reimuller
980 17th Avenue, Santa Cruz, CA 95062

Sturdi-Built Manufacturing Company
11304 S.W. Boones Ferry Road, Portland, OR 97219.

Texas Greenhouse Company
2717 St. Louis Avenue, Fort Worth, TX 76110.

Turner Greenhouses
P.O. Box 1260, Goldsboro, NC 27530.

Wooden Planter Instructions

American Plywood Association
P.O. Box 11700, Tacoma,
Washington 98411

California Redwood Association
One Lombard Street, San Francisco,
CA 94111

Periodicals and Plant Societies

These societies change officers regularly
which often creates a change in
mailing addresses. At the time of
publication the following addresses
were current.

African Violet Society of America, Inc.
Box 1326, Knoxville, TN 37901
Membership $6.00 yearly includes
African Violet Magazine 5 *times per year.*

American Begonia Society, Inc.
1431 Coronado Terrace, Los Angeles,
CA 90026
Membership $4.00 per year includes
The Begonia *monthly.*

American Fern Society
Department of Botany, University of
Tennessee Knoxville, TN 37916
Membership $5.00 per year includes
American Fern Journal *quarterly.*

**The American Gloxinia and Gesneriad
Society, Inc.**
Department AHS, P.O. Box 312, Ayer,
MA 01432
Membership $7.00 per year includes The
Gloxinian *Bi-monthly and the use of the
seed fund and library.*

**Cactus and Succulent Society
of America, Inc.**
P.O. Box 3010, Santa Barbara, CA 93105
Membership of $12.50 per year includes
Cactus and Succulent Journal *bi-monthly.*

Epiphyllum Society of America
P.O. Box 1395, Monrovia, CA 91016
Membership of $5.00 per year includes
Epiphyllum Bulletin *Bi-monthly and*
Membership Directory.

American Orchid Society, Inc.
84 Sherman Street, Cambridge, MA 02140
Membership of $15.00 per year includes
American Orchid Society Bulletin *monthly.*

**The American Plant Life Society and
The American Amaryllis Society**
Box 150, LaJolla, CA 92037
Membership $5.00 per year includes Plant
Life — Amaryllis Yearbook *bulletin.*

**The Indoor Light Gardening Society of
America, Inc.**
423 Powell Drive, Bay Village, OH 44140
*30 regional chapters Membership of $5.00
includes* Light Garden *bi-monthly.*

The Palm Society
An International Organization
1320 S. Venetian Way, Miami, FL 33139

Saintpaulia International
Box 549, Knoxville, TN 37901
Membership of $6.00 per year includes
Gesneriad—Saintpaulia News, *bi-monthly.*

American Horticultural Society
Mount Vernon, VA 22121
*Membership $15.00 per year includes
newsletter and bi-monthly magazine.*

Flower and Garden
4251 Pennsylvania, Kansas City, MO 64111
*$6.00 per year; monthly and bi-monthly.
Regionalized for Northern, Southern, and
Western areas.*

Horticulture
125 Garden Street, Marion, OH 43302
*$14.00 per year; monthly.
Informative features on all phases of
gardening.*

The Avant Gardener
P.O. Box 489, New York, NY 10028
*$15.00 semi-monthly. Digest of the latest
in horticultural events, discoveries,
products, and news.*

Books

Bringing the Outdoors In
H. Peter Loewer
Walker and Company

Exotica
Alfred Byrd Graf
Roehrs Company, Inc.

**Flowering House Plants and
Foliage House Plants**
James Underwood Crocker
Time-Life Encyclopedia of Gardening

Gardening In a Bowl
Elvin McDonald and James McNair
Doubleday

Gardening Indoors Under Lights
Frederick H. & Jacqueline L. Kranz
Viking Press

Home Orchid Growing
Rebecca Tyson Northern
Van Nostrand Reinhold Company

Houseplants for City Dwellers
Alys Sutcliffe
E. P. Dutton

Houseplants for the Purple Thumb
Maggie Baylis
101 Productions

Houseplants Indoors/Outdoors
Edited by Elvin McDonald & James McNair
Ortho Book Series

**How to Grow Beautiful House
Plants**
T. H. Everett
Fawcett

**Indoor Plant Selection and
Survival Guide**
Terrestris
Grosset & Dunlap

Lighting for Plant Growth
Elwood D. Bickford & Stuart Dunn
The Kent State University Press

Making Things Grow
Thalassa Cruso
Knopf

The Avant Gardener
Thomas and Betty Powell
Houghton Mifflin Company

**The Complete Book of Houseplants
Under Lights**
Charles Marden Fitch
Hawthorn

The Complete Book of Houseplants
Charles Marden Fitch
Hawthorn

**The Complete Book of Houseplants
Under Lights**
Charles Marden Fitch
Hawthorn

The Complete Indoor Gardener
Edited by Michael Wright
Random House

The House Plant Answer Book
Elvin McDonald
Popular Library

The World Book of House Plants
Elvin McDonald
World Publishing and Popular Library

The Indoor Light Gardening Book
George A. Elbert
Crown Publishers

Suppliers of
Artificial Lighting Accessories

Aladdin Industries, Inc.
P.O. Box 10666
Nashville, TN 37210

W. Atlee Burpee Company
Warminster, Pa 18974

Craft-House Manufacturing Company
Wilson, NY 10706

Duro-Lite Lamps, Inc.
Duro-lite Dept. PA-12
Fair Lawn, NJ 07410

Duro-Test Corporation
North Bergen, NJ 07047

Environment One
2773 Balltown Road
Schenectady, NY 12309

Fleco Industries
3347 Halifax Street
Dallas, TX 75247

Floralite Company
4124 E. Oakwood Road
Oak Creek, WI 53154

Fluorescent Tube Service
13107 South Broadway
Los Angeles, CA 90061

Garcy Corporation
Spacemaster Home Products Division
2501 N. Elston Avenue
Chicago, IL 60647

General Electric Company
Lamp Division
Nela Park
Cleveland, OH 44112

The Green House
9515 Flower Street
Bellflower, CA 90706

Grower's Supply Company
P.O. Box 1132
Ann Arbor, MI 48106

Hall Industries
2323 Commonwealth Avenue
North Chicago, IL 60064

House Plant Corner
P.O. Box 810
Oxford, MD 21654

H. L. Hubbell, Inc.
Zeeland, MI 49464

Lord & Burnham
Irvington, NY 10533

Marko
94 Porete Avenue
N. Arlington, NJ 07032

Neas Growers Supply
P.O. Box 8773
Greenville, SC 29604

George W. Park Seed Company, Inc.
Greenwood, SC 29646

Service Lighting Products
Capitol Street
Saddle Brook, NJ 07662

Shoplight Company
566 Franklin Avenue
Nutley, NJ 07110

H. P. Supplies
16337 Wayne Road
Livonia, MI 48154

Tube Craft, Inc.
1311 West 80th Street
Cleveland, OH 44102

Vend-A-Ray-Corporation
615 Front Street
Toledo, OH 43605

Blooms of Lipstick vine (*Aeschynanthus*
species) are contrasted with delicate fronds
of *Nephrolepsis exaltata* 'Elegantissima'.

Index

Numbers in italics indicate illustrations and charts. The Plant Selection Guide, pages 128-138, lists plants alphabetically by common name, with the botanical name following. It gives the growing requirements for each plant.